THE
BIBLE &
FUTURE
EVENTS

THE
BIBLE &
FUTURE
EVENTS

An Introductory Survey
of Last-Day Events

Leon J. Wood

Academie
Books Grand Rapids, Michigan
Zondervan Publishing House

Contents

Preface

Preface

The purpose of this book is to present a brief, biblical survey of last-day events from the premillennial, pretribulational point of view. Many Christians have an interest in what the future holds but lack information concerning it. This book seeks to fill that information gap by presenting an overview, briefly and simply stated.

All of the major eschatological events are discussed in chronological order. As each event is presented, the pertinent scripture passages are set forth, with the more important portions being analyzed. The Bible is the authoritative source of information, and its message must be made central in any such discussion.

Numerous terms which sometimes puzzle many Christians necessarily enter a study such as this. These are defined early in the book in chapter two. The same chapter contains a brief description of each event, so that the reader may relate these together quickly before moving into the fuller discussion of them in the following chapters. Each chapter closes with a list of review questions which the student may use to test himself on the knowledge he has gained from his reading. They may also be used for class discussion or in study groups.

The reader will find some rather detailed arguments in the book regarding the more controversial matters. These arguments may be difficult to follow and may, in fact, seem out of keeping with the more popular intent of the book. If the reader wishes to omit some or all of this argumentation, he can do so without any great loss to him in the overall view. However those who do follow it should find their thinking stimulated as to the relative merit of the view presented.

Complete bibliographical information on books cited in the footnotes is given at the end of the book.

Unless otherwise indicated, Bible references are taken from the King James Version.

THE
BIBLE &
FUTURE
EVENTS

1

Introduction

A. Significance of Prophetic Study

Some Christians do not believe that the study of prophecy is worthwhile. They see prophecy as too uncertain, and subject to too many different interpretations. They believe one is wiser to concentrate on "solid" aspects of Bible study, where conclusions are more sure, and let future events prove to be whatever happens when the time comes. Some of this thinking has been engendered through past pronouncements by interpreters who have been too specific. Dates have been set for the return of Christ, and particular people have been identified as being one or another prophetic person. When succeeding events have proven these predictions wrong, people have been disillusioned, with consequent disfavor being brought on prophetic study.

There are both good and bad features in this line of thinking. A good feature is the discrediting of that type of prophetic teaching which becomes too specific, going beyond what the Bible itself teaches. Christ Himself said that no man knows the day and hour of His coming, but the Father only (Matt. 24:36). Men are not to set dates, nor to identify predicted persons. Another good feature is that concentration on solid aspects of Bible study is advocated. The Christian cannot give himself too much to learning what the Scriptures have to say about God, man, sin, Christ, salvation, the church, etc. One bad feature, however, is that all prophetic study is discredited, as though this is not solid and as though no definite conclusions can be reached. Great vistas of prophetic truth become clear and definite when one follows careful principles of interpretation. The sacred writers would not have been led to include so much regarding last-day events if this were not true. God did not reveal His Word to confuse people; nor did He intend that substantial portions of it should be left unstudied. The Christian may approach prophetic passages with the same confidence for interpretation as he does other portions of Scripture.

Moreover, the Bible student who omits prophetic passages is overlooking the relative importance the Bible itself places on prophecy. Christ spent considerable time talking about the subject, and extensive sections in both the Old and New Testaments are devoted to it. A conservative estimate is that fully one-fourth of the Bible concerns prophecy. This emphasis on prophecy is shown also by the many times the Christian is urged to watch for Christ's coming;[1] and one who is not interested in studying the prophetic portions concerned can hardly be expected to watch.

B. Importance of Fulfilled Prophecy

The main interest of this book concerns events of the last days, which are still future. A word is in order, however, concerning events now past, which were, just as definitely, predicted beforehand. The Christian rejoices to note the exact and complete fulfillment of these predictions. He can anticipate that the same will be true concerning unfulfilled prophecies. Many of the fulfilled predictions concerned Christ's first coming. All became a matter of history when He appeared. For instance, He was born of a virgin (Isa. 7:14), at Bethlehem (Mic. 5:2), which led to a slaughter of children by Herod (Jer. 31:15). After that He was called out of Egypt (Hos. 11:1). Later He was anointed with the Spirit (Isa. 11:2), made His triumphal entry into Jerusalem (Zech. 9:9), was betrayed by a friend (Ps. 41:9) for thirty pieces of silver (Zech. 11:12), was spit upon and scourged (Isa. 50:6),

---

[1] See Matt. 24:42-44; 25:13; Luke 12:35-40; Rom. 8:23; 1 Cor. 1:7; Phil. 3:20; 1 Thess. 5:1-11; Heb. 9:28; James 5:7, 8; Rev. 16:15; et al.

but no bone of Him was broken (Ps. 34:20). He was given gall
and vinegar to drink on the cross (Ps. 69:21). His hands and
feet were pierced, His garments parted, and lots cast for His
vesture (Ps. 22:16, 18). He died in the place of sinful man (Isa.
53:4-6).

Other areas of predictions fulfilled by the time of Christ include the destruction of certain great cities of ancient time. For
instance, Nineveh's fall was predicted by both Nahum (2:8 - 3:7)
and Zephaniah (2:13, 14). Nineveh was a great city, the capital
of the mighty Assyrian empire. For all its strength, however,
the city fell in due course before the combined might of Babylonia
and Media, with the probable help of the Scythians, in 612 B.C. [2]
Nineveh was exceeded in grandeur only by Babylon, capital of
Nebuchadnezzar's empire. Babylon's walls and fortresses were
believed impregnable. But even before its greatest glory under
Nebuchadnezzar, Isaiah made bold to write, "And Babylon, the
glory of kingdoms, the beauty of the Chaldees' excellency, shall
be as when God overthrew Sodom and Gomorrah" (13:19; cf.
Jer. 51). This too came to pass, not immediately, but in God's
due time. The Persian ruler Xerxes virtually destroyed it in 478
B.C. Alexander the Great planned to restore it, but he died before doing so (323 B.C.). The few people who still lived there
in 275 B.C. moved to Seleucia, nearby on the Tigris River, and
the city came to a practical end.[3] Today, as reported by Rawlinson, "On the actual ruins of Babylon the Arabian neither
pitches his tent nor pastures his flocks—in the first place, because
the nitrous soil produces no pasture to tempt him; and secondly,
because an evil reputation attaches to the entire site, which is
thought to be the haunt of evil spirits." [4]

---

[2] For discussion, see A. T. Olmstead, *History of Assyria*, pp. 636-639;
H. W. F. Saggs, *The Greatness That Was Babylon*, pp. 138, 139. (For complete biographical information on these and other books cited in footnotes,
see Bibliography at end of book.)

[3] See John Urquhart, *The Wonders of Prophecy*, p. 138; or "Babylon,"
The Biblical World: A Dictionary of Biblical Archaeology, ed. C. Pfeiffer,
pp. 124-133.

[4] H. Rawlinson, *Egypt and Babylon*, p. 206, quoted by Urquhart in *The
Wonders of Prophecy*, p. 140. Main excavation of the site was conducted
by R. Koldewey for the German Oriental Society over a period of 18 years,
beginning in 1899. More recent work was done by Lenzen in 1956-1958.

Perhaps the most interesting story concerning fulfilled prophecy has to do with ancient Tyre. Tyre was the queen of the seas, the capital of old Phoenicia. Tyre had grown rich from trade; as her ships brought merchandise from ports near and far. Ezekiel foretold her destruction in vivid detail (26:1-21). It seemed that Nebuchadnezzar would fulfill all Ezekiel had set forth almost immediately after the prediction was given. Nebuchadnezzar did bring great destruction on the city, persisting in a continued attack over a span of thirteen years (587-574 B.C.); but he never really did capture it, nor did he draw its stones into the sea, as Ezekiel had prophesied (v. 12). At the time, one might have said that God's Word through His prophet was not proving true. The Tyrians then rebuilt their city on an island about one-half mile from shore, and became even stronger in world affairs than before. More than two centuries passed, as both pride and wealth grew. But finally God's time arrived for the complete fulfillment. It was effected by Alexander the Great in 332 B.C. As part of his overall plan to conquer the Medo-Persian empire, he determined to seize the city. To do so, he planned to construct a causeway through the sea, which would reach from shore to island; over it he would march his army. Such a causeway required great amounts of material, and Alexander used the ruins of the former mainland city to get it. Thus, as Ezekiel had predicted, the stones and the timbers and the dust of the city were indeed laid "in the midst of the water" (v. 12), and the ancient site became "like the top of a rock" (v. 14). All that God's servant had foretold was fully realized.

C. Benefits of Prophetic Study

Both daily experience and clear statements of Scripture testify that there is significant value in the study of prophetic passages. Several benefits may be listed as follows.

1. *Spiritual stimulation*

The Bible itself makes clear that a knowledge of prophecy is spiritually stimulating. That is, it prompts the Christian to lead a life pleasing to God. In First John 3:3, where the context concerns Christ's second coming, the statement is made: "Every man that hath this hope in him purifieth himself, even as he is pure." Jesus related holiness of life to the second coming in

Matthew 16:24, 27, saying, "If any man will come after me, let him deny himself, and take up his cross, and follow me"; He gave as an incentive these words, "For the Son of man shall come in the glory of his Father with his angels; and then he shall reward every man according to his works." Paul, too, in Colossians 3:4, 5, urges the Christian to mortify his "members which are upon the earth; fornication, uncleanness, inordinate affection, evil concupiscence, and covetousness, which is idolatry," giving as an incentive, "When Christ, who is our life, shall appear, then shall ye also appear with him in glory." The Scriptures further relate particular aspects of a godly life to the second coming: for instance, sobriety of life in First Thessalonians 5:2-6; First Peter 1:13; 4:7; faithfulness in service, Matthew 25:19-21; Luke 12:42-44; 19:12, 13; moderation, Philippians 4:5; patience in trial, Hebrews 10:36, 37; James 5:7, 8; personal sanctification, First Thessalonians 5:23; obedience to God, First Timothy 6:13, 14; godliness of outlook, Second Peter 3:11-13.

That there is a close relationship between a knowledge of prophecy and godliness of life may be verified further by an observation of Christians in an average church congregation. Pastors regularly testify that the most devoted and faithful workers are those who are knowledgeable concerning last-day events and look for Christ's return. Those who expect Christ to come again have a corresponding desire to live in a way which pleases Him. It is logical that a Christian would like to be found doing God's will when Christ comes again. A recognition of His imminent return also leads to a sense of closeness to Christ, which in turn leads to greater love and deeper devotion. Living in a sense of expectancy is really an integral part of the Christian experience. The New Testament writers themselves were led by the Holy Spirit to prompt Christians in their day to watch (e.g., Rom. 13:12; 1 Pet. 4:7). Expectancy of His return leads to Christ-centeredness in thinking and conduct.

2. *Mental satisfaction*

The Christian experiences mental satisfaction from knowing what the future holds. God endowed man with a mind for thinking and knowing. Man can use this wonderful instrument in ways which glorify God, or he can employ it otherwise. Those ways which glorify God the most are those which concern God Himself and His will for the world. Therefore a Christian should spend much time in Bible study, to learn about God and about God's works among men. Many of God's works have been wrought in the past, and to study these leads to a fuller recognition of the greatness and love of God. Many other works, however, lie in the future and have been predicted. God would not have revealed information concerning these works if He had not wanted man to know about them and render praise for them. As man knows of these future events and gives praise, he experiences meaningful satisfaction of mind. One feels a sense of spiritual fulfillment both by satisfying legitimate curiosity as to what the future holds and by experiencing another area of truth for which to glorify God.

3. *Psychological stabilization*

Not only is one's mind thus satisfied, but the study of prophecy also stabilizes one's emotional balance. There is a need for this in today's fast-moving world. So much that one encounters leads to frustration and disappointment. Aspects of life that one believes he can depend on one day appear quite differently the next. He can easily lose his sense of balance in judging values. On what can he rely? Where can he look for certainty and security? For the non-Christian, the future is highly threatening. Will he keep his job? Will he maintain his health? Will an accident take the life of a member of his family? Still more uncertain for him is death. Though he may try to hide these uncertainties under a facade of false confidence, yet he knows these questions are very real. The answer to them (and the peace of heart he needs so much) lies only in a saving relationship with Christ. And for one who enjoys this relationship, a knowledge of future events, as revealed in the Bible, is vital for providing the full sense of peace and security desired. No matter what life may hold today, the Christian can know the main outlines in God's program of last-day events and that in those events his personal welfare is secure. (See Rev. 2:25; 3:11.)

4. *Comfort in sorrow*

The Bible speaks frequently of the comfort which a knowledge of prophecy affords the suffering Christian. This suffering often takes the form of bereavement for a loved one who has died. The person then senses a great loss, missing the companionship formerly enjoyed. But true comfort is available in the knowledge that the one departed has gone to be with the Lord and a sure reunion will one day be experienced.

Paul speaks of this truth in First Thessalonians 4:16-18:

> For the Lord himself shall descend from heaven with a shout, with the voice of the archangel, and with the trump of God: and the dead in Christ shall rise first: Then we which are alive and remain shall be caught up together with them in the clouds, to meet the Lord in the air: and so shall we ever be with the Lord. Wherefore comfort one another with these words.

Suffering can also take the form of persecution. A knowledge of Christ's coming gives comfort when one experiences oppression and hardship of this kind. It lets the Christian know that deliverance from the persecution can come at any time. Of this truth Peter says, "But rejoice, inasmuch as ye are partakers of Christ's sufferings: that, when his glory shall be revealed, ye may be glad also with exceeding joy" (1 Pet. 4:13; cf. 1:7).

Still a third form of suffering is slander and misunderstanding. A person may easily be hurt in social relationships, either intentionally or unintentionally. The wound may be deep, but again comfort is available in knowing that one day the full truth of all such matters will be brought to light, "and then shall every man have praise of God" (1 Cor. 4:5). The result can and should be joy in place of sorrow, as one anticipates the appearing of the Savior. This truth was a clear factor in the mind of Jesus when He promised the disciples that, though He was about to leave them, He would prepare a place in heaven for them and would return to take them there to be with Him (John 14:3).

5. *Conviction for service*

The recognition of Christ's return for His church leads the Christian also to a conviction regarding service for God. This conviction is closely related to the desire for holiness of life. The Christian is prompted not only to live properly, but to serve diligently. He sees the need of getting busy for God, so that his friends and loved ones may hear the Gospel and be saved. He is also motivated to prepare to appear before the judgment seat of Christ. Paul speaks of this in Second Corinthians 5:9, 10: "Wherefore we labour, that, whether present or absent, we may be accepted of him. For we must all appear before the judgment seat of Christ; that every one may receive the things done in his body, according to that he hath done, whether it be good or bad." (Cf. 2 Tim. 4:1, 2.)

A knowledge of last-day events gives the Christian a new evaluation regarding the best use of his time. This leads to his giving more time for service. He also can anticipate joy at having served, when the Savior comes for His own. Paul speaks of a "crown of righteousness" laid up for all those who "love his appearing" (2 Tim. 4:8). Peter promises a "crown of glory that fadeth not away" to church leaders who do their work well (1 Pet. 5:2-4; cf. Matt. 19:28). Joy at seeing Christ Himself, as well as hearing His approval for work well done, will make the moment of His appearance a happy one indeed. Anticipating that moment provides a definite incentive for serving well during the time of waiting.

D. Signs of the Times

Though the Bible states definitely that the exact date of Christ's second coming is beyond man's knowledge, it does set forth signs of that coming, that the Christian may be alerted to the time in general. What is more, it urges the Christian to be aware of those signs. Jesus rebuked the Pharisees of His day for not recognizing the signs which indicated His presence among them (Matt. 16:3) — signs such as His lowly birth, His miracles, His being a man of sorrows and acquainted with grief, His riding into Jerusalem on a colt, etc. It seems logical that He would similarly rebuke Christians today for not being alert to signs of His second coming. He gave a number of those signs, some more general in nature and others surprisingly specific and unique. Many of the more general signs are set forth in Matthew 24:6-12: "wars and rumors of wars," "famines, and pestilences, and earthquakes," persecution of Christians, betrayal by friends, the appearance of false prophets, and the abounding of iniquity. These signs are quite general in type and have appeared at various times throughout history since Christ's first coming. They all exist today, in this latter half of the twentieth century, probably to a degree more pronounced than at any prior time, suggesting the proximity of Christ's return.

A specific sign which is surely more pronounced today than in any prior century, is that of apostasy within the so-called

Christian church. Paul, writing to Timothy, said that "in the latter times some shall depart from the faith, giving heed to seducing spirits, and doctrines of devils" (1 Tim. 4:1). He said also that in the last days men would be "lovers of pleasures more than lovers of God, having a form of godliness, but denying the power thereof" (2 Tim. 3:1-5). Prior centuries have known some measure of apostasy, as people have turned from the true faith, but not to the degree existent today. This apostasy does not concern merely peripheral issues either, but the most central of all: the very supernaturalism of Christ and the Bible. Christ has been declared merely a man, though a remarkable one, and the Bible merely a human product, though again an unusually valuable one. This liberal form of theology started with the rise of rationalism in Germany, spread across to England, then to the United States, and finally throughout the world. Theological schools, individual churches, and even whole denominations have fallen before its onrushing tide. Never before in history has anything like it occurred in the area of theology. It is truly a mark of the imminence of last-day events.

E. The Clear Sign of the Modern State of Israel

The clearest sign of Christ's return is the modern state of Israel. The Scriptures teach that in the last days Jews will return to their land in large numbers, with a resultant reestablishment of their sovereign state. For instance, Isaiah states:

> And it shall come to pass in that day, that the Lord shall set his hand again the second time to recover the remnant of his people, which shall be left. . . . And he shall set up an ensign for the nations, and shall assemble the outcasts of Israel, and gather together the dispersed of Judah from the four corners of the earth (11:11, 12).

The first return implied in this passage, was from Babylon in 538-537 B.C., when the people of Judah came back to Palestine from one direction, the east. But the second return, says the prophet, will be from the "four corners," or the four directions. No instance of such a return occurred until the twentieth century, which means that the one witnessed now must be the one predicted. And Jews have indeed been returning in this day from each of the four directions. They have come from as many as one hundred different countries.

The Scriptures also say that, having returned to the land, the people will not be forced to leave again. Amos states: "And I will bring again the captivity of my people of Israel. . . . And I will plant them upon their land, and they shall no more be pulled up out of their land which I have given them, saith the LORD thy God" (9:14, 15). Since the Jews were forced to leave Palestine again after the first return, the return Amos predicted must be the present return, the one foretold by Isaiah. It is very probable, therefore, that the nation of Israel now existing will remain, and that this return is indeed the lasting one which the Scriptures say will immediately precede the beginning of last-day events.

The fulfillment of these promises concerning Israel began to occur at the close of the nineteenth century. Zionism, the movement which has effected the present existence of Israel as a state, began under the direction of Dr. Theodore Herzl. Beginning in 1897, a series of Zionist congresses was held to explore ways to create a homeland for Jews in Palestine. The great majority of Jews had been out of the land since the two times when Roman legions smashed Jewish revolutions, A.D. 70 and A.D. 132. Little was accomplished by these congresses, however, until Great Britain's General Allenby, as part of an overall plan of the Allies in World War I, conquered Palestine. Turkey had held the land since the days of its great Ottoman empire, and was adverse to the idea of Palestine becoming a homeland for Jews. At the time of Allenby's victory, the attitude of Great Britain was quite different. It was expressed in an official letter written by Lord Balfour, which read in part:

> His Majesty's Government views with favour the establishment in Palestine of a national home for the Jewish people, and will use their best endeavours to facilitate the achievement of this object, it being clearly understood that nothing shall be done which may prejudice the civil and religious rights of existing non-Jewish communities in Palestine, or the rights and political status enjoyed by Jews in any other country.

This change to a governmental control sympathetic to Zionism gave encouragement to Jews the world over, and the next two decades saw a great increase in Jewish population in Palestine. In 1882, there had been approximately 24,000 Jews in Palestine, out of a total population of 624,000. By 1914, under the impetus of what the early Zionist congresses had been able to accomplish, this number had risen to 85,000. In 1927 it reached 150,000; in 1936, 404,000; and in 1948, when the modern state was born, 650,000.

This growth was not without opposition from the Arab populace. The former inhabitants saw their influence waning under the more energetic activity of the Jews. Strife between the two groups increased as the years passed. In 1939, British policy toward the Jews was officially altered and migration quotas were severely limited. This change was felt especially after the close of World War II, when so many Jews, desiring to flee from Germany following the Nazi atrocities, wanted to enter Palestine. Boatloads left southern European ports, the passengers hoping somehow to make entrance to the land of promise; but most were disappointed. Strife was severe within the land, as the British sought to maintain their new policy, and the Jews sought just as diligently to circumvent it. Finally the United Nations attempted to solve the problem by a plan of partition. Areas of greatest Jewish population were identified and designated as belonging to the Jews, with the remainder of Palestine assigned to Jordan. The United Nations voted on 29 November 1947, and the vote was 33 to 10, with 10 abstentions, in favor of the plan. The Jews were pleased, but the Arabs, who wanted the Jews to receive no land at all, were not. As a result, the Arabs initiated planned warfare on a scale exceeding anything before. Six months of attack and retaliation, with consequent loss of many lives and much property, followed. Finally, Great Britain withdrew from the scene on 14 May 1948, at which time the Jews declared themselves a sovereign state, in accordance with the United Nations vote.

With this declaration of independence, fighting became even more intense. The Arabs were determined to drive all Jews into the Mediterranean Sea, as they themselves said. The withdrawing British were quite convinced that this would, in fact, occur; but, amazingly, it did not. Though troops from Egypt, Jordan, Syria, Lebanon, and Iraq entered formally into the fray, the stubborn Jews, fighting for their dream of centuries, were able to withstand the attack and gradually begin to win on the various fronts. Then the tide definitely turned, and Israel, after a series of cease-fires, which were successively broken by the Arabs, gained substantial portions of land which had been assigned to the Arabs. The result was that, when a new line of partition was drawn, the boundaries now included much more territory for Israel than those of the original partition. These boundaries continued until the Six Day War of 1967, when Israel seized control of large areas of Arab land. About 8000 square miles were included in the assigned portion after 1948; this increased to four times that amount after 1967. The most important prize of the Six Day War was the possession of all Jerusalem, with access to the sacred site, the Wailing Wall, as well as control over the Temple area. This brought the realization of the promised rebuilding of the Temple a definite step closer.

The modern state of Israel is now a reality in the world. The student of prophecy need no longer say merely that this will happen some day, but that it has already happened. This is one of the clearest and most unmistakable signs that the last-day events are near at hand. One should still be cautious, of course, and avoid being too specific. One should realize that God's timetable could call for Israel to be in the land for many years before bringing the fruition of the age. But with the nation actually there, and with many factors concerning it fitting into conditions set forth in Scripture for the last days, as will be seen, one may safely believe that Christ's coming is not far in the future.

F. Understanding Prophecy

One reason some Christians remain uninterested in prophetic study is that they believe the passages concerned are too difficult to interpret. The symbolism often used in these passages seems puzzling, and certainty as to the meaning appears quite impossible. This is a mistaken attitude, however, for, as noted above, God would not have included so much in His Word concerning future events if the information was not understandable. When Christ spoke the farewell discourse to His disciples, He included a specific promise in this connection, saying, "Howbeit when he, the Spirit of truth, is come, he will guide you into all truth . . . and he will shew you things to come" (John 16:13). Christ quite clearly realized that the "things to come" prophesied in the Bible could be difficult to recognize and understand, and He wanted to give Christians the reassurance that in this area, too, His

Spirit would lead them. This means that one should study prophecy with confidence, claiming this promise of the Savior. As one does so, however, he will be helped by observing a few rules of interpretation.

1. *Interpret the passage literally*

One should interpret prophetic passages as literally as he does other scripture portions. God did not prophesy for the purpose of hiding His message. He did not intend that only certain Christians, who had some special key of interpretation, should be able to understand it. He set forth truth so that it might be known. This means that prophetic portions are to be studied in the same manner as other passages, employing literal, common-sense principles of interpretation. This does not mean that figures of speech should not be expected and recognized. Many types of scripture portions use figures of speech. Figures enliven and illustrate the truth presented. But these are recognizable without difficulty, in prophetic passages as well as others, and the text itself shows them to be what they are. The figure itself must be understood symbolically, but this symbolism, in turn, will be of something literal.

For instance, Isaiah predicted that "there shall come forth a rod out of the stem of Jesse, and a Branch shall grow out of his roots" (11:1). "Rod" and "Branch" here are figurative expressions, but the Person whom they symbolize is very literal. The literal interpretation is that Christ, as this "Rod" and "Branch," would arise in literal, historical fashion and do the things set forth in the remainder of the passage.

The amillennial school of prophecy [5] denies this principle of interpretation, holding instead to the principle of "spiritualization." That is, adherents of the view, though they use the literal approach for other portions of Scripture, believe that prophetic passages must be understood "spiritually." By this is meant that such passages are to be interpreted as symbolizing church-oriented truth. For instance, the prediction that Christ will rule over Israel is said to mean that He will rule over His church. All passages, then, which speak of this rule of Christ should be interpreted in the sense that Christ will establish not an earthly rule over Israel in Palestine after the pattern of Old Testament kings, but a spiri-

---

[5] See chapter 2, p. 29, for identification.

tual rule in the hearts of those belonging to His church. It seems fair to say that the principal reason for this spiritualization is that a literal interpretation of these portions appears to amillennialists as absurd. Christ just would not rule here on earth in a literal manner.

In response to this type of thinking, it may be pointed out that prophecies of Christ's first coming were all fulfilled in a literal, historical manner. Some of these must have seemed quite absurd at the time: for example the virgin birth, the miracles, the crucifixion, and the resurrection. But history has proven that they were not intended to be taken symbolically; and adequate reason does not exist for believing those regarding His second coming are so intended either.

The error in prophetic spiritualization may be further demonstrated by noting briefly a particular passage. In Luke 1:31-33, the angel Gabriel addresses Mary in reference to the birth of Jesus. He states that Mary will conceive and bear a son, who should be called Jesus, and that He would be great and would be called "Son of the Highest"; and then he adds the words, "The Lord God shall give unto him the throne of his father David: And he shall reign over the house of Jacob for ever" (literally, "unto the ages"). The whole passage is of one piece, with no clue that any part is to be interpreted on different principles than another. The amillennialist, however, takes the first part, in reference to Christ's birth, literally and the second part, in reference to his rule, spiritually.

2. Recognize the possibility of a time interval

Some prophetic passages intermingle references to future events, which may themselves be widely separated as to time of fulfillment, so that the time interval between them is not recognized. In such passages, the sacred writer, as he foresaw these events in his day, viewed them in the distance of time like peaks of a mountain range, without realizing that valleys of time lay between them. This is true especially concerning events in the first and second advents of Christ. A clear example is found in Isaiah 61:1, 2, which Christ read in the synagogue of Nazareth (Luke 4:16-21). The major part of the passage predicts aspects of Christ's first advent including His being anointed "to preach good tidings unto the meek, . . . to bind up the brokenhearted, to proclaim liberty to the captives, and the opening of the prison to them that are bound; to proclaim the acceptable year of the Lord." The last part of the passage, however, which is grammatically parallel to the first, refers to Christ's second advent, namely, the phrase, "And the day of vengeance of our God; to comfort all that mourn." Here, then, references in respect to the two advents, which are separated by at least two millennia of time, are included in one passage, and no clue is given there of that lapse of time. Jesus Himself, when He read the portion, gave evidence of the lapse by including in his reading only that portion, which had to do with the first advent, significantly adding the words, "This day is this scripture fulfilled in your ears." When the interpreter comes to a portion similarly characterized, he must recognize the time interval involved. A comparison with other prophetic passages, where the time distinction is identified, especially in the later revelations of the New Testament, will provide the help needed.

3. *Recognize the possibility of a double reference*

Not only may two different prophetic times be talked about in one passage, but the same words may carry reference to more than one time of fulfillment. That is, there may be an earlier partial fulfillment and a later complete fulfillment. This fact is sometimes identified as the law of double reference in prophecy. A good example may be taken from Isaiah's prediction concerning a sign to be given to Ahaz. The sign was needed as a way of reassuring Ahaz that God would shortly deliver Jerusalem from a siege by the kings of Israel and Syria. The prophet identified the sign as the birth of a child; before the child would know good from evil, the deliverance would be effected (Isa. 7:14-16). This prophecy must have been fulfilled already in Ahaz' day for it to have been meaningful as a sign to him. This fulfillment is best identified with the birth of Isaiah's own son, Maher-shalal-hash-baz (Isa. 8:1-4). This could not have been the complete fulfillment, however, because the child to be born would be the child of a virgin, and his name would be called Immanuel. This complete fulfillment came only with Christ, as Matthew 1:22, 23 clearly states. The interpreter of prophecy must recognize the possibility of similar double references in other passages and discern their meaning accordingly.

Questions for Review

1. What should be the attitude of Christians toward the study of predictive prophecy?
2. Is it beneficial to study unfulfilled prophecy as one studies that which has been fulfilled?
3. Name three great ancient cities whose destructions were predicted in the Old Testament.
4. Describe briefly five benefits of prophetic study.
5. What should be the attitude of Christians toward signs of the times?
6. Name some of the more general signs of the last days listed by Jesus.
7. In what way is present-day religious apostasy a clear sign of the times?
8. What is probably the clearest sign of the imminent return of Christ?
9. When did the modern movement of Zionism begin?
10. What was the significance for Zionism of General Allenby's campaign in World War I?
11. What was the attitude of Great Britain, following Allenby's victory, toward the hopes of Zionism?
12. What decision in respect to Palestine did the United Nations make on 29 November 1947?
13. How much land was included in Israel's border after the victory of 1948?
14. How much was added in 1967?
15. Should a Christian enter upon prophetic study confident of being able to understand it? Tell why.
16. What is meant by a literal interpretation of prophecy?
17. What is meant by the "spiritualization" of prophetic passages?
18. What principle of interpretation is illustrated in Isaiah 61:1, 2?
19. What is meant by a double reference in predictive prophecy?

2

The
Overall
View

A. Definition of Terms

Before proceeding to deal with specific aspects of the last-day events, it is well to look at the overall sequence in one view. In turn, before looking at this general survey, there is benefit in defining some basic terms.

1. The *rapture* of the church is the taking up of the redeemed from this world by Christ just prior to the beginning of the tribulation period.

2. The *judgment seat of Christ* is the place where Christ judges Christians, immediately after their rapture, on the basis of their conduct as Christians, resulting in a receiving of rewards by some and a sense of loss for others.

3. The *marriage supper of the Lamb* is a term used in Revelation 19:7-10 to refer to the specific occasion, occurring sometime between the rapture and the revelation of Christ, when the church is eternally united to Christ as His bride.

4. The *great tribulation* is a period of seven years, beginning shortly after the rapture, when judgment is meted out upon the world at large for its sinfulness of past ages. At this time the restored nation of Israel is tried by the fire of suffering to bring the Jews to a receptive attitude toward Christ as their

Messiah-Deliverer. Because the last half of this period is more severe in the degree of suffering experienced, the term is often used in reference only to the last three-and-a-half years of the total seven.

5. The *revelation of Christ* is a term commonly used to designate the return of Christ to the earth at the conclusion of the great tribulation, when He comes with the saints of the church, raptured seven years before, to bring deliverance for Israel which is being oppressed by the Antichrist.

6. The *battle of Armageddon,* a name taken from Revelation 16:16, designates the battle in Israel which brings the great tribulation to a climax, as the Antichrist triumphs over the Jews to seize Israel's homeland for himself. Part of the struggle, probably its beginning, takes place at the historic battle scene of Megiddo, well north of Jerusalem, but descriptive passages show it will end at Jerusalem.

7. The *judgment of Gentiles* is an occasion of judgment, immediately following the time of Christ's deliverance of Israel from the Antichrist, when a determination is made regarding which Gentiles will be permitted to enter the millennial period. The criterion for judgment will be personal righteousness as believers in Christ, evidenced by the attitude of each shown during the great tribulation toward Christ's "brethren," the Jews.

8. The *millennium* is a period of one thousand years, beginning soon after the judgment of Gentiles, when Christ rules in perfect righteousness and continual peace over the state of Israel, in particular, and over all the world, in general, with resurrected saints, now glorified, acting as assistants in this rule.

9. The *great white throne judgment* follows the millennium and is the occasion when the unsaved of all ages will receive their sentence of eternal punishment in hell for their sin.

10. The *premillennial view* of last things holds to the existence of a literal, earthly millenium, as just defined, and believes that the rapture of the church precedes it.

11. The *postmillennial view* holds to the existence of a literal millennium, resulting from the spread of the Gospel and the salvation of a vast number of people, with Christ returning to the earth at its conclusion.

12. The *amillennial view,* denying the existence of a literal millennium, sees the millennial promises as being fulfilled in a spiritual kingdom; some adherents hold that this kingdom is Christ's rule over His church here on earth and others that it is God's rule over the saints in heaven.

13. The *pretribulational view* holds that the rapture of the church will be not only premillennial but pretribulational; that is, it will occur before the beginning of the great tribulation, meaning that the church will not experience this severe period of suffering.

14. The *posttribulational view* agrees with the pretribulational view that the rapture will be premillennial, but holds that it will occur *after* the great tribulation, meaning that the church will be on earth during this seven-year period.

15. The *midtribulational view* also agrees that the rapture will be premillennial but disagrees in holding that it will occur at the midpoint of the great tribulation, meaning that the church will not experience the last half of this period when suffering will be the most severe.

B. Sequence of Events

The sequence of last-day events, as held by pretribulational premillennialists, will now be set forth. It is important to keep this sequence clearly in mind, so that the many features involved, which are discussed at greater length in the following chapters, may be better understood and interrelated as they are presented.

1. *The rapture of the church*

The first occurrence in the sequence of last-day events is the rapture of the church. Christ will come to meet the church, His bride, in the air (1 Thess. 4:17), without descending all the way to the earth's surface at the time. Christians then living will be caught up to meet Him and given glorified bodies at the same instant (1 Cor. 15:52-54). These glorified bodies will be constituted after the fashion of Christ's resurrected body (1 John 3:2), not being limited to all the laws of nature as are our present bodies (Luke 24:31; John 20:19, 26; Acts 1:9). Those who have died in Christ will be raised from the dead and given glorified bodies, that they too may meet Christ in the air, preceding the living Christians (1 Thess. 4:16, 17). This resurrection will include only saints of the church and will be an aspect of what is called the "first resurrection" (Rev. 20:5, 6); two other aspects will occur later. The saints of the church thus united with Christ will be with Him in heaven during the seven years of tribulation on earth.

During this time, two principal events will take place in heaven involving these saints. The first is their judgment by Christ, before what is called the "judgment seat of Christ" (Rom. 14:10; 2 Cor. 5:10). The issue involved will not be salvation, for only those who are already saved will be there. At issue will be their works as Christians, "the things done in the body" (2 Cor. 5:10), to distinguish between those works which are good and acceptable and those which are bad and rejected.[1] The former will be rewarded, but the latter will result in a sense of loss for the person (1 Cor. 3:14, 15). The second event will be the marriage of Christ and the church, at what is called the "marriage supper of the Lamb" (Rev. 19:9), when the church, now judged, will be eternally united to Christ as His bride.

2. *The great tribulation*

The period called the great tribulation (Matt. 24:21) will ensue shortly after the rapture, though some time may elapse between to allow for certain necessary developments. These developments would include, for example, the restoration of the Roman confederacy and the appearance of the Antichrist as the confederacy's ruler (2 Thess. 2:3). The period will last seven years, as shown by its identification with Daniel's seventieth week (Dan. 9:27). During this time a series of catastrophic punishments will be brought on the world, symbolized by broken seals (Rev. 6:1-17), blown trumpets (Rev. 8:1 - 9:21; 11:15-19), and poured-out "vials of the wrath of God" (Rev. 16:1-21).

These punishments, which will work enormous havoc, will be meant especially for the Gentile world as retribution for its continued rejection of God and His will through all ages. The Jews of Israel will likely be spared in large part from these punishments (Isa. 26:20, 21), but they will experience severe oppression at the hand of the Antichrist during the last half of the period, an oppression called "the time of Jacob's trouble"

---

[1] In 1 Corinthians 3:12, the first group of works is likened to gold, silver, precious stones, and the second to wood, hay, stubble.

(Jer. 30:7). The Antichrist will make a covenant with them (Dan. 9:27) at the beginning of the seven-year period, promising a period of rest and peace; but at the midpoint he will break this covenant as he orders sacrifices and offerings to cease at the Temple (restored by this time). He then will become as much their enemy as before he was their friend. He will conquer all their land, including the city of Jerusalem (Zech. 14:2) and will even be able to establish a residence there (Dan. 11:45). The horror he brings will result in the destruction of no less than two-thirds of the Jewish populace (Zech. 13:8, 9). This suffering is permitted by God as a means of refining the Jews, "as silver is refined, and . . . as gold is tried" (Zech. 13:9), so that they will be made ready to receive Christ as their Messiah and King when He comes to deliver them from the Antichrist (Zech. 14: 3, 4; Rev. 19:11-21).

3. *The revelation of Christ*

This deliverance by Christ will occur when the Antichrist has been fully victorious over Israel. The army of the Antichrist is said to be in the "valley of Jehoshaphat" (Joel 3:12) at the time, probably relaxing after the battle. This valley is best identified with the Kidron Valley, lying at the foot of the Mount of Olives, dividing the mountain from Jerusalem. In full view of this army, Christ will come in a display of power (2 Thess. 1: 7, 8; Rev. 19:14, 15) to the Mount of Olives, which will split open at the time (Zech. 14:4). His first act will be to cast both the Antichrist and his chief assistant, the False Prophet (Rev. 13: 11-18), into the lake of fire (Rev. 19:20). He then will slay all their vast army, quartered in the valley (Rev. 19:21). The Jews of Jerusalem will be first-hand witnesses of this destruction, and this will prompt them in unison to accept Christ as their Deliverer and King. At this point in the sequence, several events will transpire which call for individual notice.

a. Judgment of the Gentiles.[2] One of these events is Christ's judgment of Gentiles, conducted here on earth (Matt. 25:31-46). The judgment will be on an individual basis, and the criterion will be the attitude of each person in respect to the Jews, the "breth-

---

[2] The description of an accompanying judgment of Jews is included in the fuller discussion in chapter 8.

ren" of Christ (Matt. 25:40). Those who were friendly to them will be called sheep and will be placed at Christ's right hand, and those who were unfriendly will be called goats and will be placed at His left hand (Matt. 25:32, 33). Because those called goats will be assigned eventually to everlasting punishment (Matt. 25: 46), this outward attitude toward Jews must be reckoned as evidence of an inward attitude toward Christ. That is, those who are friendly thereby demonstrate personal faith in Christ, and those not friendly show their lack of faith. This conclusion follows because the remainder of Scripture clearly states that one's attitude toward Christ is the final criterion as to one's eternal state. This is evidenced also from the recognition of the kind of people who will be willing to be friendly to the Jews. One must remember that the Jews will be the oppressed people of the time, persecuted by the Antichrist. Only Gentiles who have put their trust in Christ will show sufficient conviction and courage to act the part of a true friend. Those judged to be sheep will be given the privilege of entering the millennial period, which means that a prime purpose of this time of judgment will be the determination of those to be granted this blessing.

b. *Resurrection of Old Testament and tribulation saints.* A second event at this time is another resurrection of saints. This occasion is still called the "first resurrection" (Rev. 20:4-6), because it concerns saints and not unbelievers. The second resurrection, corresponding to the "second death" of Revelation 20: 6, 14, in which unbelievers are involved, will not occur until after the millennium. Those resurrected in this second aspect of the first resurrection will be tribulation saints, those who have died after having been saved during the tribulation (Rev. 6:9), and also Old Testament saints, who quite clearly will not be raised with church saints at the rapture. Daniel, an Old Testament saint, is told that he will stand in his "lot at the end of the days" (Dan. 12:13; cf. 12:2). This means that he will rise from the dead to receive his assigned lot, or status, at the end of the days discussed in the immediately preceding context, namely the days of the tribulation. Both groups will receive glorified bodies at the time and join with returned church saints to assist Christ in His rule of the world (Rev. 20:4).

c. *Binding of Satan.* Satan will be unusually active during the tribulation period, working directly through the Antichrist

(2 Thess. 2:9; Rev. 13:2), who is also called the "man of sin" (2 Thess. 2:3). However, he will be bound and completely restricted from exercising any influence during Christ's millennial rule (Rev. 20:1-3). He will be cast into a place of confinement, called the "bottomless pit," from which he will be permitted no access to the minds of men. With his work thus halted during this thousand-year period, and with Christ serving as the righteous King of all the earth, "the earth shall be full of the knowledge of the LORD, as the waters cover the sea" (Isa. 11:9).

d. Establishment of the kingdom. The millennial kingdom will also be established at this time. Numerous matters will call for attention as the inauguration is anticipated. For instance, the boundaries of the nation of Israel, "from the river of Egypt unto the great river, the river Euphrates" (Gen. 15:18), will have to be defined. This will not be difficult at the time, however, with all opposing powers now defeated and Christ in complete authority over the world. In addition, appointments of glorified saints to their respective positions of rule will be made.

4. *The millennium*

With these matters effected, the glorious period of the millennium will begin. In this historical period of time God's pleasure will truly be carried out in the world; and, as a result, both Israel in particular and the Gentile world in general will enjoy the blessed manner of life which both could have had in past days if they had conducted themselves in God's will. During this thousand-year period, Christ will rule as the sovereign King, and under Him will be three groups of people as His subjects. First will be the host of glorified saints, those who have returned with Christ as His church and those who have just been raised from the dead as tribulation or Old Testament saints. These people, ruling with Christ and having glorified bodies, will not be limited by many of the normal physical restrictions of earth, even as Christ was not after He received His glorified body (John 20: 19, 26; Acts 1:9). Second will be the nation of Israel, composed of Jews who will have accepted Christ as their Messiah-King. Their number will be made up of those who have placed personal trust in Him during the tribulation and those who have been persuaded to render this allegiance by Christ's deliverance at its close. Third will be the Gentile populace throughout the world, who have been declared proper millennial participants by Christ at the judgment of Gentiles.

The last two groups will be constituted of normal people, who have not died and have not received glorified bodies. They will carry on their lives just as at any time in history, except for the presence of righteousness in place of sin. They will marry, have families, hold jobs, and die, as generation follows generation through the extended thousand-year time. At first they will number comparatively few, but as the generations pass, with long life spans (see Isa. 65:20) and, likely, large families, their number will increase rapidly. Under such favorable conditions, the population, by the close of the period could easily approximate or exceed that of the present day. The great majority of children born will be led to exercise faith in Christ, because the influence for good will be as strong then as it is today for wickedness. There is reason to believe, however, that a few will be rebellious, which will call for the rod of Christ to be employed (Ps. 2:9; Isa. 11:4). It will be from these, apparently, that Satan will be able to find sufficient recruits at the end of the millennium to make one last but unsuccessful try to gain world control (Rev. 20:7-9). People of the earth will enjoy constant blessing during the time, and the nation of Israel will be the leading world power (Deut. 28:1-14).

5. *The great white throne judgment*

The second resurrection occurs after the millennium and will include the unsaved of all ages. They will be made to stand before "a great white throne" for judgment. The location of this throne will apparently be somewhere between heaven and earth, for Revelation 20:11 states that "the earth and the heaven fled away" from before the face of Him who sat on the throne. The purpose of the occasion is to judge the evil deeds of the unsaved and pronounce a sentence of eternal death upon them. All will be cast into hell, where there will be eternal separation from God and unending suffering.

A third aspect of the first resurrection will occur at this same general time. This will involve saints who have died during the millennium. The Scriptures do not speak specifically of this time of resurrection, but logical deduction indicates that it will happen. If these saints are to have glorified bodies in the eternal state following, which surely will be true, they must arise at this time to receive them.

C. A Brief History of Principal Views

Various viewpoints regarding last-day events have been held through the centuries of church history. There is value in noting the principal ones. The evidence for a given view is not made stronger because it was held earlier than another, or by more people; but confidence may be gained by the adherent of a view if he knows that other Bible students, through significant periods of history, have held it.

1. *The first two centuries of church history*

There is general agreement among scholars that the view of the early church was premillennial. That is, Christians held that Christ would rule over a literal, earthly kingdom for one thousand years, assisted by raptured saints. No church fathers of the first two centuries are known to have disagreed with this view. The following may be listed as those who favored it: from the first century, Aristio, John the Presbyter, Clement of Rome, Barnabus, Hermas, Ignatius, Polycarp, and Papias; from the second, Pothinus, Justin Martyr, Melito, Hegisippus, Tatian, Irenaeus, Tertullian, and Hippolytus. [3] Though not all of these set forth their view with the same clarity, some gave very clear indications of their premillennial position. Two of these are particularly significant. First is Papias (A.D. 80-163), who not only stated his own view clearly but added that his view was held also by the apostles Andrew, Peter, Philip, Thomas, James, John, and Matthew. Papias was in a position to know early church thinking, for Irenaeus says of him that he was one of John's hearers and was intimate with Polycarp. It may be concluded that, in the early church, a common view was that Christ's apostles were themselves premillennial. Second is Justin Martyr, of the second century, who not only set forth his own premillennial position but added that this was the view of all Christians who were orthodox.

2. *The third century*

In the third century the premillennial view continued to be held by many. Peters [4] lists the following among those who did: Cyprian, Commodian, Nepos, Coracion, Victorinus, Methodius,

---

[3] George Peters, *The Theocratic Kingdom,* I, pp. 494-496.
[4] Ibid.

and Lactantius. At the same time, this century witnessed the rise of opposition to the view. Leaders in this were Gaius, Clement of Alexandria, Origen, and Dionysius. This opposition grew out of a new approach in hermeneutics. The allegorical method of interpreting Scripture was made to replace the former literal method; and, since the premillennial position found its basis in literal principles, it soon came into disfavor. In all fairness, it should be added that no true adherent of present-day amillennialism (which also rejects the literal interpretation of millennial passages) accepts the allegorical method then set forth.

3. *The fourth century*

It is generally agreed that the fourth century saw the decline of premillennial thinking. Few voices were now being raised in its favor. Instead, theologians came to interpret millennial concepts as symbolic of church-related truths. The beginnings of amillennial thinking can be discerned in this. Peters[5] cites the following factors which he believes contributed to this change of view. First, several erroneous doctrines arose, such as Gnosticism, Asceticism, and Docetism, which could not be reconciled with the idea of a future earthly kingdom. Second, Judaism, having begun already in the early church, now gained strength, which resulted in greater enmity between Jewish and Gentile Christians. This, in turn, tended toward a denial of the millennium since the millennium had a distinctly Jewish character. Third, Emperor Constantine made Christianity the official religion of Rome, which resulted in a loss of expectancy among Christians for the return of Christ since the church was no longer being persecuted. Many Christians believed that this temporal supremacy of Christianity was the actual fulfillment of the millennial promises, an opinion voiced officially by Rome itself.

4. *The rise of amillennialism*

Though the earliest beginnings of amillennial thinking can be traced back to the third century, Augustine (A.D. 354-430) is properly credited as the first to systematize this non-literal view of the millennium. He was a highly capable theologian, and his thinking came to carry great weight in all doctrinal discussion of

---

[5] Ibid., pp. 500-505.

the Roman Church after his day. He set forth his view particularly in his well-known volume, *The City of God,* in which he advocated that the visible church was the kingdom of God on earth. He believed that the millennium should be interpreted spiritually as fulfilled in the church. He believed that the binding of Satan occurred during Christ's earthly ministry, that the first resurrection should be identified with the new birth of the believer, and that the millennium, therefore, must coincide with the present church age. With the Roman Church accepting this viewpoint, it became the dominant position for centuries, though certain groups, outside the mother church and considered heretical at the time, did continue to hold to premillennial tenets. Among these were the Waldenses, the Paulicians, and the Albigenses. [6]

5. *The rise of postmillennialism*

The leaders of the Reformation continued in amillennial thinking, though it should be recognized that they gave little of their attention to last-day matters. Their main concern was rightly. with the area of salvation, where they had their main differences with the Roman Church. A matter of note is that they called for a return to the literal method of interpretation, and this, quite apart from their intention, really laid the foundation for a return to premillennialism. It was not premillennialism that first brought a change in eschatological thinking, however, but a new view which came to be called postmillennialism. Daniel Whitby, (1638-1726), a liberal Unitarian, is generally considered the originator of the viewpoint. Some of his basic ideas, however, had been presented as early as the twelfth century by Joachim of Floris. [7] Whitby saw a wonderful age for the church in the future, climaxed by a man-made millennium. Other liberals followed him, attracted by the suitability of the view to the evident progress of man in society, science, and technology. Conservative Bible students were attracted also, for the view returned to the idea of an earthly kingdom, which was felt to be more in keeping with numerous Scripture passages. As a result, both a liberal and a conservative type of post-millennialism came into being; the former

---

[6] See Charles Ryrie, *The Basis of the Premillennial Faith,* pp. 27, 28; also Peters, *The Theocratic Kingdom,* I, p. 521.

[7] H. Kromminga, *The Millennium in the Church,* p. 20.

seeing man making his own millennium by natural progress, and the latter viewing the millennium as the result of an increasing number of people being saved through faith in Christ. Postmillennialism became widely accepted among leading theologians. It was dealt a severe blow, however, by the two World Wars of this century, which showed that man was not making the progress that had been envisioned.

6. *Revival of premillennialism*

Along with the rise of postmillennialism came a less noticed return to premillennialism, following the early days of the Reformation. This resulted, as already noted, from the return to literal principles of interpretation. The movement was slow in developing at first, but it gradually gained impetus as men of recognized stature were persuaded in favor of it. Among these were the following: Bengel, Steir, Alford, Lange, Meyer, Fausset, Bonar, Ryle, Tregelles, Lightfoot, and Darby. Due to the leadership and influence of such men, the last century has seen the view come to the fore. It may be added that amillennialism has experienced a strong revival also, with the diminishing influence of postmillennialism. At the present time the two leading positions are premillennialism and amillennialism.

Questions for Review

1. Tell what the following terms mean:

   rapture
   judgment seat of Christ
   marriage supper of the
       Lamb
   great tribulation
   revelation of Christ
   battle of Armageddon
   judgment of Gentiles

   millennium
   great white throne judgment
   premillennial view
   postmillennial view
   amillennial view
   pretribulational view
   posttribulational view
   midtribulational view

2. Where will resurrected saints meet Christ at the rapture?
3. What two developments may intervene between the rapture and the beginning of the tribulation period?
4. What purpose will the tribulation period serve for Gentiles?
5. What purpose will it serve for Jews?
6. What happens to the Antichrist, the False Prophet, and their army at the revelation of Christ?
7. What test will be used by Christ to judge the Gentiles?
8. When will Old Testament and tribulation saints be resurrected?
9. What is the significance of Satan being bound during the millennium?
10. What matters will have to be disposed of by Christ as He anticipates the inauguration of the kingdom?
11. What three general groups of people will be subjects during Christ's millennial rule?
12. Will any sinful, rebellious people live during the millennium? Give a reason for your answer.
13. What two groups of people will be resurrected after the millennium?
14. What was the prevailing view regarding the future during the first two centuries of church history?
15. What bearing did the advocacy during the third century of the allegorical view of interpreting Scripture have on this prevailing view?
16. What view came into vogue during the fourth century?
17. What viewpoint was held by Augustine?
18. What two types of postmillennialism came to existence?
19. What two viewpoints regarding last things are most commonly held today?

3

The
Rapture

The first in the series of last-day events is the rapture of the church. The rapture begins the last-day period. There is no way to know when it will occur, but, when it does, the other events can be expected to follow in a predictable schedule. This means that the rapture is the occasion for which the church looks, and it could happen at any time. No event is known which must happen before it occurs, and, as noted in chapter one, numerous indications signify that it could well be in the near future.

A. Mentioned in Scripture

In keeping with its importance, the rapture is mentioned frequently in Scripture. It is well to note some of the more significant passages as a beginning point in the discussion. Jesus spoke of it as He began His closing message to His disciples, just before the crucifixion, saying, "I will come again, and receive you unto myself; that where I am, there ye may be also" (John 14:3). The scene was the upper room, with the Lord's Supper having just been instituted. Jesus spoke of leaving His disciples shortly and of going to prepare a place for them, meaning heaven. Then He voiced these important words, that He would come to get them that they might be with Him in that place so prepared. The passage reveals several things regarding the rapture.

One is that it is a planned event; at the time of His departure Christ anticipated returning for the disciples. Another is that it concerns Christ's own, His followers. Christ was speaking only to the disciples when He gave the promise. Third, Christ's return for His own will be personal. He Himself will come for them, not sending some angel, for instance, nor merely giving a general permission for the church finally to come to Him. Fourth, the rapture results in the church being taken out of the world. Jesus said that He would come and "receive" the disciples, that there where He had made the preparations, they might be also. The church will not remain here on earth, then, merely in some improved status, but will be taken away from the earth to heaven.

Another important passage is First Corinthians 1:7, where Paul refers to the rapture with the words, "Waiting for the coming of our Lord Jesus Christ." He uses that thought as a basis for urging the Corinthian Christians to "come behind in no gift," as they seek to live for and serve God. Paul thus says that the expectancy of the rapture provides a reason for the Christian's total life being dedicated to God. Paul's main thought is to urge this kind of dedication. His reference to the rapture shows that it should motivate the Christian to this end.

In Philippians 3:20 Paul writes of the rapture as the time when Christians will be taken to the place of their true citizenship. This passage reads, "For our conversation [citizenship] is in heaven; from whence also we look for the Saviour, the Lord Jesus Christ." The thought is that, since the Christian's final home is heaven and not this troubled world, he looks forward to going there. Since the rapture is the occasion when he will be taken there, it is made the more important to him.

The writer of Hebrews mentions the rapture as he contrasts the purpose of Christ's second coming with that of His first coming. He states, "So Christ was once offered to bear the sins of men; and unto them that look for him shall he appear the second time without sin unto salvation" (Heb. 9:28). The thought is that Christ came the first time to pay the penalty of man's sin, but the second time He will come to effect man's deliverance from the world. The phrase, "without sin," does not imply that Christ had sin in His first coming, of course; but in the second coming He will not be involved with sin in any way, as He was the first time in bearing man's sin. The rapture, then, will be the time when Christ delivers the Christian out of the world unto Himself.

The same writer refers to the rapture again as a reason for hope on the part of suffering Christians. He states, "For yet a little while, and he that shall come will come, and will not tarry" (Heb. 10:37). The rapture is a source of true comfort for every child of God, knowing that, no matter the degree or kind of suffering one may experience here on earth, Christ is coming to bring deliverance.

B. Distinguished From the Revelation of Christ

Christ's coming at the rapture must be distinguished from His coming at what is commonly called His revelation. The latter appearance will not occur until after the tribulation period, and will be for a different reason. The revelation appearance is dis-, cussed more fully in chapter eight. There is value here, however, in listing some basic distinctions between the two comings. First, the revelation does not occur until after the tribulation, rather than before as does the rapture. This is indicated, for example, in Matthew 24:29, 30. This means that the two appearances are separated by no less than seven years. Second, the revelation is described as a coming "in flaming fire taking vengeance on them that know not God" (2 Thess. 1:8). This presents an entirely different picture from His coming graciously to receive His church unto Himself. Third, He comes in the revelation *with* His saints, rather than *for* them, as at the rapture. Jude 14, for instance, states, "Behold, the Lord cometh with ten thousands of his saints." Fourth, at the revelation, Christ descends fully to the earth, coming to the Mount of Olives (Zech. 14:4) from which He ascended when He went back to glory. At the rapture, however, He descends only far enough to meet the saints in the air (1 Thess. 4:17).

C. Described in First Thessalonians 4:13-18

One of the fullest treatments of the rapture is found in First Thessalonians 4:13-18. This passage calls for special attention.

When Paul wrote his first epistle to the Thessalonians, he had not been away from them more than a few weeks. He had been forced to leave them hastily due to persecution (Acts 17:1-10), later had spent a short time in Berea (Acts 17:10-14), then had gone on to Athens (Acts 17:15-34), and finally had come to Corinth, where he wrote the book. Timothy and Silas had come to him recently from Thessalonica (Acts 18:5; 1 Thess. 3:6) and had reported some anxiety among the saints concerning those of their number who had died, perhaps in the continuing persecution within the city. Their question concerned the status of these at the time of Christ's coming. They seem to have been at ease regarding their own prospect of being taken to heaven at the time but they were not sure how matters would work out regarding the dead.

Paul sets forth the answer in First Thessalonians 4. He begins by assuring them that they have no need to be anxious (v. 13). All those "which sleep in Jesus" will be caught up to meet the Lord at the rapture, even before those still living. This will involve their resurrection from the dead, an event which will be similar to the resurrection of the Lord Himself (v. 14). Paul then gives the assurance, which is "by the word of the Lord," that those still living at the time will not even "precede" (a better translation than "prevent," as in the King James Version) them which are asleep (v. 15). Rather, "the Lord himself shall descend from heaven with a shout, with the voice of the archangel, and with the trump of God, and the dead in Christ shall rise first" (v. 16). Then those "which are alive and remain shall be caught up together with them in the clouds, to meet the Lord in the air" (v. 17).

Some additional facts regarding the rapture should be noticed. One is that a resurrection will be involved, a time when those who have previously died in Christ will be raised. Another is that those resurrected will be caught up to meet Christ prior to those still living. Further, both the raised dead and the living will meet Christ in the air and not somewhere on the earth's surface. Still further, this coming of Christ will be accompanied by audible signs, namely, "a shout," "the voice of the archangel," and "the trump of God." The word translated "shout," is used only here in the New Testament, and it means a "word of command." It may here refer to Christ's command, mentioned in John 5:28, 29, for those in the graves to "come forth." Since only Michael is called by the term "archangel" in Scripture (Jude 9), he is probably the one who accompanies Christ and is responsible for the "voice" mentioned. Perhaps he utters a voice of triumph at the event about to transpire. The "trump of God" is best identified with "the last trump" mentioned in First Corinthians 15:52, both expressions likely referring to a trumpet sound of deliverance. Sometimes Christians use the designation "secret rapture." The term is somewhat misleading, however, for, though the time is unknown beforehand, these audible signs will occur. Certainly all saints will hear them, and it is likely that the unsaved will as well. The signs would let the unsaved know of the significant occurrence and that they have indeed been left out.

D. The Resurrection of Church Saints

The idea of resurrection in the last days is frequently mentioned in the Scriptures. A few passages refer to the resurrection of both the just and the unjust in a way seeming to suggest that both groups will be raised at the same time. For example, Jesus states, "Marvel not at this; for the hour is coming, in the which all that are in the graves shall hear his voice, and shall come forth; they that have done good, unto the resurrection of life; and they that have done evil, unto the resurrection of damnation" (John 5: 28, 29; cf. Acts 24:15). Other passages, however, where the context calls for more detail, refer only to one or the other group being raised at a particular time. That is the case in the passage just studied, First Thessalonians 4:13-18, where the reference is only to the "dead in Christ" with no mention of the unsaved dead. It is the case also in Revelation 20:13, where reference is to the other group, the unsaved. This passage states, "And the sea gave up the dead which were in it; and death and hell delivered up the dead which were in them: and they were judged every man according to their works." This resurrection clearly follows Christ's millennial reign, because a description of that great time immediately precedes these words. Also, this occasion of resurrection is connected with what is called the "second death" (v. 14), which earlier in the chapter (v. 6) is said to have no power over those of the first resurrection. The two groups, then, are raised at different times.

Another distinction as to times of resurrection must be made, one which pertains only to the saved dead. One group of the saved will be raised at the rapture, as noted, but two other groups will be raised at two later times. One of these will be raised at the close of the tribulation period. This group will include those who are saved and die during the tribulation and also saints from Old Testament centuries. (Discussion of pertinent scripture passages is included in chapter eight.) The other group will be raised at the close of the millennium. It will consist of saints who died during that thousand-year period. The Scriptures do not speak specifically of this resurrection, but the inference is clear enough. If millennial saints are to have a part in eternal blessings, along with saints of prior ages, there will have to be a time of resurrection for them as for the others.

The idea of such a sequence of resurrections is set forth in First Corinthians 15:20-24, where Paul speaks of Christ's own resurrection and then states that in the same pattern "shall all be made alive." He immediately explains that this will be according to a schedule: "every man in his own order." That is, all will not be made alive at the same time. Christ is the "firstfruits," the pattern for the rest, and others will follow in a planned sequence. Actually, two other resurrections of righteous follow Christ's resurrection. One has happened, namely, the resurrection of saints immediately after Christ's death. Matthew tells of the occasion: "And the graves were opened; and many bodies of the saints which slept arose, and came out of the graves after his resurrection, and went into the holy city, and appeared unto many" (Matt. 27:52, 53). The purpose of this resurrection was apparently to provide a further credential in support of Christ's resurrection. Those raised likely were people who had died not long before and were well known by acquaintances still living. What an impression must have been made as these departed ones were seen, alive and well, walking through the streets of Jerusalem! It is commonly believed that these people did not die again, as did, for instance, Lazarus and others raised under totally different circumstances. They probably were taken directly to heaven after performing the mission intended in their resurrection.

The other occasion of resurrection will yet occur, namely that of the "two witnesses" who will live and die during the tribulation period (Rev. 11:3-12). These two people will witness for God in Israel for 1,260 days and then will be killed by "the beast" (the Antichrist) at the close of that time. Their bodies will lie openly on the streets of Jerusalem for three-and-a-half days, since no one will dare or be willing to bury them. At the close of these days, they will suddenly be brought to life, after which they will ascend directly to heaven. [1]

---

[1] For discussion, see chapter 7, pp. 130-133.

The resurrection at the rapture, then, is one aspect in this series of resurrections. At this time those raised will be the church saints, that is, all who have been saved during the period of the church, from its beginning on the day of Pentecost until the moment of rapture. The number of people involved will be very large, much larger, for instance, than the number of living saints at the time, who will be translated without dying. The latter group will include only the one generation then alive, while the resurrected saints will include all the many generations since the early first century. This time of resurrection is an occasion every Christian can anticipate with joy, for at that time he will see departed loved ones again as well as the great saints of past days.

E. Glorified Bodies

The righteous will receive glorified bodies at the time of their resurrection. Nothing is said in the Scriptures regarding raised bodies of the unsaved, but much is said regarding bodies of the righteous, a fact which is in keeping with the distinction already noted between the two occasions. Paul refers to the change of body for the righteous, as he says that we who "have the firstfruits of the spirit . . . groan within ourselves, waiting for the adoption, to wit, the redemption of our body" (Rom. 8:23). That is, saints, whose spirits have experienced renewal, anticipate eagerly the time when their bodies will also be made anew. In this life, the body still acts as a hindrance to the redeemed spirit. It needs the change which the resurrection will provide.

The subject is treated at length in First Corinthians 15:35-54. Paul begins by raising the question, "How are the dead raised up? and with what body do they come?" Then he describes that body. In verse 42 he says that it will be an incorruptible body, not subject to decomposition; in verse 43, he says that it will be a body of "glory" (i.e., honored by God and free from effects of the curse), and of "power" (i.e., not subject to weakness, weariness, or disease); and in verse 44, he points out that it will be a "spiritual body," meaning that though it will be very real, it will not be subject to all the natural limitations of present bodies, which require nourishment, rest, medical care, etc. Following this description Paul states, in verses 51, 52, that also those yet living will receive glorified bodies, but through sudden change rather than resurrection. This will occur, he says, "in a moment, in the twinkling of an eye." He adds that these changed bodies will be incorruptible and immortal (v. 53).

Perhaps the greatest help in understanding the nature of glorified bodies comes from Paul's statement that God will "change our vile body, that it may be fashioned like unto his glorious body" (Phil. 3:21; cf. 1 John 3:2). Glorified bodies, then, will be like Christ's resurrected body. In that body, Christ could enter a room when the door was shut (John 20:19, 26); vanish from sight while talking with others (Luke 24:30, 31); remain unknown to others until special perception was granted (Luke 24:15, 16, 31; John 20:15, 16); and defy gravity in ascending from the earth to disappear in the clouds (Acts 1:9). At the same time, His body was real, for it could be touched (John 20:27), was capable of speaking (Luke 24:17-32), and quite clearly could consume food (Luke 24:30; John 21:12-15). Glorified bodies, then, will be real and physical, but will not be subject to death and decay; they will not become weary or sick; they will not need food for sustenance, though being capable of eating on occasion; and they will not be limited by either ordinary physical matter or natural laws, being able to vanish and appear at will and to defy gravity for upward movement. Since Christ at His ascension apparently moved from earth to heaven with the speed of thought, this too will no doubt be possible for glorified saints. The saints of the church will be endowed with such bodies at the rapture, moving up in them to meet Christ in the air.

F. Sudden and Unannounced

Christ's coming for His church will be sudden and unannounced. No advance warning will be given. Christians will not be able to make up for lost time in their service or become occupied at the last moment with spiritual interests. Neither will the unsaved have a final period in which to turn to Christ. Christ's return will catch people doing normal things in normal ways. This is made clear in several scripture portions, such as Jesus' account of servants waiting for the return of their lord who was away at a wedding (Luke 12:36-38). Jesus says, "Blessed are those servants, whom the lord when he cometh shall find watching . . . " whether "he shall come in the second watch, or come in the third watch."

Jesus follows this story with that of a thief coming to break and enter a house. He says, "If the goodman of the house had known what hour the thief would come, he would have watched, and not have suffered his house to be broken through" (v. 39). Thieves do not give advance notice. The householder needs to be prepared at all times. Jesus admonishes, "Be ye therefore ready also; for the Son of man cometh at an hour when ye think not" (v. 40).

In a parallel passage, Jesus compares the time of His coming with the time of Noah (Luke 17:26, 27). As the flood caught people unprepared (they were occupied in eating and drinking and giving themselves to a life of sin), so it will be at Christ's coming. He compares it also with the time of Lot (Luke 17:28, 29), stating that, as fire and brimstone caught the people of Sodom totally unprepared and "destroyed them all," so will it be "when the Son of man is revealed." He states further that, at the time of His coming, there shall be "two men in one bed; the one shall be taken, and the other shall be left. Two women shall be grinding together; the one shall be taken, and the other left" (Luke 17:34-36). Jesus was saying pointedly that all men need to be ready for Christ's coming beforehand, so that last-minute preparations will not have to be made. The unsaved need to be saved, while they have the opportunity; and Christians need to be busy for the Lord, truly living for Him at all times, so that they will not be ashamed when they see Him.

G. The Judgment Seat of Christ

"The judgment seat of Christ," a time of judgment for raptured saints, will take place shortly after the initial meeting with the Savior. The issue will not concern the saved or lost state of those being judged, for only those already belonging to the church will be judged at this time. No one will be present who does not trust Christ as personal Savior and who has not been justified by the Father. The issue will concern, rather, the life-conduct of each person since he became a Christian.

The term used in Scripture in reference to this occasion is "the judgment seat of Christ"; it is employed in both Second Corinthians 5:10 and Romans 14:10.[2] The "judgment seat" (Greek, *bema*) of the Greek and Roman world was a tribunal where a

---

[2] In Romans 14:10, the best reading is "the judgment seat of God," but this difference is of little, if any, significance.

judge sat. The word *bema* is used, for instance, of the place where Pilate sat when he made pronouncement concerning Christ (Matt. 27:19; John 19:13) and of the place where Gallio sat when Paul was brought before him in Corinth (Acts 18:12, 16; cf. 25: 6). The judgment seat of Christ, then, will be the place where Christ pronounces judgment on the raptured, glorified saints of the church.

1. The necessity of the judgment

The Scriptures are clear that all men, whether saved or lost, are accountable to God. This means that there must be a time of judgment for every person. The judgment seat of Christ is where this will occur for the saved. Several passages indicate the need for this time of judgment. In Matthew 12:36, Jesus says that "every idle word that men shall speak" shall be called into account; this is a general statement probably referring to both saved and lost people. In Galatians 6:7, Paul lays down the principle that all men must reap what they sow. Then, in Colossians 3:24, 25, Paul speaks particularly of Christians when he says that those who serve the Lord well will "receive the reward of the inheritance," but those who do wrong will receive for the wrong they have done.

Further, both of the texts mentioned, which specifically identify the occasion, are significant. Romans 14:10-12 says that "every one of us shall give account of himself to God," referring clearly to Christians. This indicates that no one will be excepted in this matter. Second Corinthians 5:10 expresses the same thought with the words: "We must all appear before the judgment seat of Christ; that every one may receive the things done in his body, according to that he has done, whether it be good or bad."

2. The time of the judgment

The time of this judgment of Christians is best placed shortly after the rapture and certainly sometime within the seven-year period of the tribulation. This is supported, first, by logical deduction. If Christians are to be judged for works done prior to the rapture, it is reasonable to believe that such a judgment would follow the rapture as soon as possible. It seems logical to let those judged know the results of their judgment sooner rather than later. Second, in Luke 14:14, Jesus states that the recompense for works done will be meted out "at the resurrection of the just," and this occasion occurs, as has been seen, at the time of the rapture. Third, both First Corinthians 4:5 and Revelation 22:12 indicate that Christ will bestow rewards at the time of His coming for His own, with the implication that this will happen at a moment very near that time.

3. *The results of the judgment*

The results of the judgment will be either a reward for works approved or a sense of loss for those not approved. This is made clear especially by Paul's treatment of the subject in First Corinthians 3:9-15. Here he talks about building materials of two classes: "gold, silver, precious stones," which are not subject to destruction by fire, and "wood, hay, stubble," which are. He states that the "labourers together with God" may build with materials from either class in their work for Him; but the fire of judgment will reveal of which class they are. Those whose works are of the first class "shall receive a reward," but those whose works prove to be of the second by burning in the fire of judgment "shall suffer loss." The criterion for judging will be the good pleasure of God. Those labors which please Him, the works which make a proper contribution to "God's building," will be declared "gold, silver, precious stones"; but those which displease Him, which do not so contribute, will be judged "wood, hay, stubble."

The nature of the rewards given for the approved works is not described in this passage, but parallel passages suggest that the rewards will be in the form of "crowns." Five distinct "crowns" are distinguished in various texts: (1) an "incorruptible crown" for those who keep the old nature in subjection (1 Cor. 9:25); (2) a "crown of rejoicing" for those who bring others to Christ (1 Thess. 2:19); (3) a "crown of righteousness" for those who love Christ's appearing (2 Tim. 4:8); (4) a "crown of life" for those who maintain their love for the Lord in the midst of trials (James 1:12); and (5) a "crown of glory" for those who are good shepherds of God's flock (1 Pet. 5:4). Whether these are all the types of crowns that will be rewarded or whether they are only representative is not revealed. It is certain, of course, that God will reward equitably, according to what each person deserves.

The loss experienced by those whose labors are burned does not concern the person's salvation. Paul makes this clear in the passage discussed, as he adds the words, "But he himself shall be saved; yet so as by fire" (1 Cor. 3:15). Rather, the loss concerns rewards. The person will not receive a crown, and this will result in a sense of shame and loss that he did not better use his time on earth. Paul seems to have foreseen such a possibility for himself and strongly wished to avoid it, when he wrote, "I keep under my body, and bring it into subjection: lest that by any means, when I have preached to others, I myself should be a castaway" (1 Cor. 9:27). He was not speaking of losing his salvation, for this cannot be lost, but of losing his usefulness in the construction of "God's building" and, as a result, losing his reward. Every Christian should consider carefully the fact of this coming time of judgment. A wasted life will seem very foolish when one stands before Christ in that day.

H. The Marriage Supper of the Lamb

There is a second event which occurs for church saints shortly after the rapture. In Revelation 17:7-9 this is referred to as "the marriage supper of the Lamb." At this supper Christ will be the Bridegroom and the church will be His bride. The figures of a bridegroom and a bride in reference to Christ and His church are frequently used elsewhere in the New Testament (see, for example, John 3:29; Rom. 7:4; 2 Cor. 11:2; Eph. 5:25-33). The marriage supper will celebrate the formal union of Christ and His church in an eternal relationship. Until this time they will have been separated, the One in heaven and the other on earth, but from this moment on they will always be together.

1. *The time of the marriage*

The time of this marriage will fall somewhere between the rapture and Christ's posttribulational return to earth. It will not precede the rapture, for until that time the separation between the two parties continues. It will not follow the posttribulational return either, because, first, the description of the marriage supper is recorded before that of the return in Revelation 19:11-21, and, second, the church, at that time of return, comes with Christ as His bride. It probably follows the judgment before Christ's "judgment seat," because at the marriage supper the church will be arrayed in "the righteousness of saints." This suggests that this righteousness has already been judged and found valid. The time of the marriage cannot be established more specifically than this, however. The fact that its description in Revelation 19 comes just before that of Christ's return to earth may be significant. On the other hand, logic points to an earlier time, shortly after the judgment; since the church will be in Christ's presence from the time of judgment on, there would not seem to be any reason for delay. All that can be said for sure is that it occurs sometime between the judgment and the posttribulational return.

2. *A possible distinction*

Some prophetic students make a distinction between this occasion, which they call "the marriage of the Lamb," and a later one, which they call "the marriage supper of the Lamb." [3] The reason for this distinction is found especially in three passages which describe a marriage feast: Matthew 22:1-14; 25:1-13; and Luke 14:16-24. The explanation is that these accounts picture Israel on earth waiting for the return from heaven of Christ, as the Bridegroom, and the church, as His bride, so that the marriage feast might take place. Thus the marriage supper is seen to take place here on earth during the millennium. The marriage itself, which is identified with "the marriage of the Lamb" (Rev. 19: 7-9), will have already taken place by the time of Christ's coming. According to this view, it will be only after this coming that the feast in celebration of the marriage will ensue. Only Christ and the church will be involved, then, in the marriage proper, but Israel will additionally act as guests at the later supper. I view this interpretation as possible, but not probable. The matter hinges on the significance of the three "feast" passages. It seems likely that they are better understood, not as predictive of a specific historical event, but merely as revealing truth under the symbolism of a marriage supper, without identifying any particular time or period for that occasion. Arguing against the interpretation, also, is the fact that the event described in Revelation 19:7-9 is already called "the marriage supper of the Lamb" (v. 9).

---

[3] See J. D. Pentecost, *Things to Come*, pp. 227, 228; Lewis Sperry Chafer, *Systematic Theology*, IV, p. 396.

Questions for Review

1. At what point does the rapture occur in the sequence of last-day events?
2. What four truths are taught concerning the rapture in John 14:2, 3?
3. List four main differences between the rapture and the revelation of Christ.
4. In what respect were the Thessalonian Christians concerned regarding those of their number who had died?
5. List the principal truths taught in First Thessalonians 4:13-18 regarding the rapture.
6. Give scriptural reasons for believing that the resurrection of the unsaved is distinct from and will follow the resurrection of the saved.
7. Which resurrection precedes the great tribulation and which one follows it?
8. What does First Corinthians 15:20-24 teach concerning resurrections?
9. What was the nature and purpose of the resurrection which accompanied Christ's death?
10. Tell all you can regarding glorified bodies, which Christians will receive at their resurrection.
11. Summarize what Luke 12:36-38 and 17:26-36 teach regarding the coming of Christ.
12. What will occur at the "judgment seat of Christ"?
13. Identify, with scriptural evidence, when this judgment will take place.
14. What does First Corinthians 3:9-15 teach concerning the results of this judgment?
15. List, with Scripture, the five "crowns" distinguished in Scripture.
16. What do the words mean, "But he himself shall be saved, yet so as by fire" (1 Cor. 3:15)?
17. What will be the purpose of the "marriage supper of the Lamb"?
18. Show from Scripture when this marriage supper will occur.
19. Why do some prophetic students make a distinction between "the marriage of the Lamb" and "the marriage supper of the Lamb"?

4

The Great
Tribulation

While the raptured church is in heaven, a time of great tribulation, lasting seven years, will take place on earth. The Scriptures have much to say concerning this period.

A. Scriptural Designations

Biblical references to this period are usually made in one of two characteristic ways.

1. *As the most severe time of trouble in history*

There are four classic scripture passages which speak of the time as being more severe in suffering than any other in history. Because there can be only one such time, all four must refer to the same period. The best known of the four is in the New Testament, and uses the designation "great tribulation" for the time. It reads: "For then shall be great tribulation, such as was not since the beginning of the world to this time, no, nor ever shall be" (Matt. 24:21; cf. Mark 13:19). The other three passages are in the Old Testament. One is Jeremiah 30:7, which reads, "Alas! for that day is great, so that none is like it." A second is Daniel 12:1: ". . . and there shall be a time of trouble, such as never was since there was a nation even to that same time." And the third is Joel 2:2: "A day of darkness and of gloominess . . . there hath not been ever the like, neither shall be any more after it."

2. As "the day of the Lord"

Many other scripture passages refer to this period as "the day of the LORD." Because of the importance of this term, some discussion is needed.

The term occurs frequently in both the Old and New Testaments: in the Old as "the day of the LORD [*Yahweh*]" (see Isa. 2:12; 13:6, 9; Ezek. 13:5; 30:3; Joel 1:15; 2:1, 11; Amos 5: 18, 20; Obad. 15; Zeph. 1:7, 14; Zech. 14:1; Mal. 4:5), and in the New as "the day of the Lord [*kuriou*]" (see Acts 2:20; 1 Thess. 5:2; 2 Thess. 2:2; 2 Pet. 3:10). A shorter form, "the day," "that day," or "the great day," occurs even more frequently and in contexts sufficiently similar to know that the same time is often in view. The thought in such passages normally pertains to punishment and suffering, through which God's wrath in judgment is being poured out.

In Old Testament texts, which pertain to pre-captivity days, the occasion of suffering often carries both a near and a far reference. That is, two occasions are foreseen when the suffering predicted will be experienced: one in the near future and one in the distant future, with the latter being the more severe. The suffering of the near future is usually the Babylonian captivity, and that of the far future, the great tribulation. Normally the text prophesies kinds of suffering which were not fulfilled in the first occasion; this calls for some future fulfillment. Or the text may describe a glorious day, following that time of suffering, which was not fully experienced by Israel in her Old Testament return from the captivity; and this again calls for a future fulfillment.

Joel 2 illustrates the latter case. Here the prophet, after speaking of "the day of the LORD" at some length sets forth several characteristics of a day of glory which will follow the period of suffering. He says in that day God will "no more make [Israel] a reproach among the heathen" (v. 19); Israel will instead "eat in plenty, and be satisfied, and praise the name of the LORD"; the nation will "never be ashamed," but will know that God is "in the midst of Israel," and that He is the Lord (vv. 26, 27). These prophecies have not been truly realized by Israel since the Babylonian captivity; and, therefore, a future day has to exist when they will be, because God's Word must be fulfilled in every detail. The glorious day, to which this passage refers, will be the millennium, which follows the tribulation period. After enduring this time of suffering Israel will enjoy the glory of the millennium and will experience fully the promises set forth.

At this point it should be made clear that the term "day of the LORD" is sometimes used in reference to another occasion of judgment in the last-day events. That occasion will immediately follow the tribulation period, when Christ comes in vengeance to bring deliverance from Israel's enemies. As will be seen later, especially in chapter seven, Israel will suffer terribly at the hand of the Antichrist during the tribulation, but Christ will come to destroy him and his hosts at the close of that time. That occasion of destruction is the time in view here. The devastation wrought will be most severe, marking it as another occasion when God pours out His wrath in judgment. This time will be comparatively brief, in comparison with the seven years of the tribulation. The context of a given passage indicates which of the two "days" is in view there; sometimes the reference is general enough to include both.

B. Rationale for the Period

According to the Scriptures two main purposes are served by the tribulation period.

1. *Retribution on the world*

One purpose is the bringing of retribution on the nations of the world for their sinfulness. All men individually have been sinners; and all nations, as collections of individuals, have likewise followed in ways not pleasing to God. The world has never witnessed the blessed existence possible on the earth, because sin has prevented the gracious benefits God has in store. One day this blessedness will be experienced, when Christ rules in justice and perfection during the millennial age. Before that time comes, however, there must be a reckoning, a time of retribution for the nations of earth. Revelation 3:10 speaks of that time as "the hour of temptation, which shall come upon all the world, to try them that dwell upon the earth." In Psalm 2:5, after first telling of the continued opposition of the nations to God and His will, the psalmist states, "Then shall he [God] speak unto them in his wrath, and vex them in his sore displeasure"; following this, significantly, the writer refers directly to the millennial age.

2. *"The time of Jacob's trouble"*

The other purpose of the tribulation is the preparation of Israel to receive her Messiah. God's people must be brought to a frame of mind receptive to their Messiah. The Jews were not ready to receive Christ the first time He came, and they are not ready today. A change is needed, therefore; this change will make them ready to accept the One they have so long rejected. However, only a major experience can bring about such a change. This is the reason for the extreme suffering of the tribulation time. Jeremiah expresses this thought in his description of the tribulation as "the time of Jacob's trouble" (30:7). Zechariah speaks of the degree of suffering involved in most somber tones, as he states, "And it shall come to pass, that in all the land, saith the LORD, two parts therein shall be cut off and die; but the third shall be left therein" (13:8). Two-thirds of the people will be cut off from the land, a devastation that defies full understanding, because nothing like it has ever been witnessed before. Zechariah then states the significance of this devastation, as he says, "And I [God] will bring the third part through the fire, and will refine them as silver is refined, and will try them as gold is tried." Finally Zechariah tells of the end accomplished by this shattering experience: "They shall call on my name, and I will hear them: I will say, It is my people; and they shall say, The LORD is my God" (13:9).

C. Duration of the Period

The tribulation period is often designated as the tribulation week. This term comes from Daniel's vision of the seventy weeks (Dan. 9:20-27); the tribulation period is identified with the seventieth of those weeks. Since the duration of the period is derived in large part from this identification, we should discuss the vision and show the propriety of the designation.

1. *Daniel's vision of the seventy weeks*

The vision is set forth in Daniel 9. In verses 3-19, Daniel prays that God will forgive the sin of his people and that God might be pleased soon to bring the seventy-year captivity in Babylonia to a close. In verses 20-23, the angel Gabriel appears to the praying prophet to convey God's response to this prayer. The response does not come in the form of a direct answer to

Daniel's request, but as a statement concerning God's future plans for the Jews. The return from captivity is implied, however, because it would be necessary in order to effect the plans. The plans call for a period of seventy weeks, in which certain matters will be accomplished. These weeks are not weeks of days, but weeks of years. The Hebrew word translated "weeks" simply means "sevens," and is applicable to sevens of years just as well as sevens of days. The Jews were really quite familiar with the idea of sevens of years, because of the sabbatical year, which came at the end of every period of seven years (see Exod. 23: 10, 11; Lev. 25). In fact, the Jews were familiar with the idea of seventy "weeks" of years, because the seventy-year captivity, coming to an end when Daniel received this vision, had to be a seventy-week period of time. These seventy years had to make up for the preceding seventy sabbatical years that had not been observed, due to disobedience on the part of the people (see Lev. 26:34, 35; 2 Chron. 36:21).

Explaining what would happen during these seventy weeks of years (490 years), the angel first describes two divisions of the seventy, a group of seven and a group of sixty-two weeks; the completion of the total sixty-nine (483 years) would culminate in the appearance of the Messiah (v. 25). After the completion of these sixty-nine weeks two events will occur: the cutting off of the Messiah, which is a reference to Christ's crucifixion, and the destruction of "the city and the sanctuary," a reference to the destruction of Jerusalem and the Temple in A.D. 70, some forty years after the crucifixion. It is only after the description of these two events that the angel comes to the third division of the total period, the seventieth week. This is the week of significance for this discussion, the one identified with the tribulation period. If this identification is correct, a long gap in time must be placed between the first sixty-nine weeks and this last week, a gap extending from Christ's first coming until the beginning of the tribulation period. Numerous evidences exist in support of this gap.

2. *Seven evidences for the time gap*

The first of these evidences is that the seventieth week is treated in the text quite apart from the sixty-nine weeks. This suggests something different about it, such as a separation in time. The second is that, since the forty years, falling between the crucifixion and the destruction of Jerusalem, are implied as intervening between the two periods, the idea of a time gap, at least of some length, is introduced by the text itself. The third is that a time gap of a length comparable to that called for here is implied in all three of Daniel's other visions; [1] thus it is not strange to find the same thing here. The fourth is that this vision of Daniel, concerning the weeks, has already implied the existence of a time gap. In verse 24, six items are mentioned as being accomplished in the seventy-week period; these concern both Christ's first coming and His second. [2] The fifth is that in Matthew 24:15 (cf. Mark 13:14), Jesus mentions the "abomination of desolation, spoken of by Daniel the prophet," as a feature of the tribulation period; that phrase is a later part of the same verse we are considering (Dan. 9:27). Jesus thus refers to this verse as involving the tribulation. The sixth is that the alternative interpretation, set forth by amillennialists, which identifies this seventieth week with Christ's ministry at His first coming, does not fit the history involved. Christ did not minister for seven years; nor is there a logical stopping point at three and one-half years after His death, if His death is taken as the midpoint of the seven years. The seventh evidence is that the description following in this verse, which concerns developments during the seventieth week, does fit the character of the tribulation week very well, as will appear.

3. *The division of the tribulation week*

In view of these evidences, one may properly conclude that Daniel's seventieth week can be identified with the tribulation period which fixes its duration solidly as seven years. Note further that this period is divided into two equal halves of three-and-a-half years each, as established by this passage. In Daniel 9:27, Gabriel states that at the beginning of the seventieth week, a covenant [3] of some type will be confirmed, which is probably a mutual-respect, non-aggression treaty between the Antichrist and Israel. [4] Such an agreement would insure a time of peace for

---

[1] See John F. Walvoord, *Daniel, the Key to Prophetic Revelation*, or Leon Wood, *A Commentary on Daniel*, for evidence.

[2] See Walvoord, ibid; or Wood, ibid.

[3] The Hebrew speaks only of "a covenant," not "the covenant," as the word is translated in the King James Version.

[4] See chapter 7, pp. 116-118, for discussion.

Israel. At the midpoint of the week, however, this covenant will be broken. The Antichrist will cause the Israelite sacrifices and offerings to cease and then will follow this by bringing a time of severe trouble. This means that the week will be divided into a first half of peace for Israel and a second half of trouble. It is this second half to which Jeremiah's term, "time of Jacob's trouble," applies.

D. Unprecedented Suffering

The degree of suffering permitted to come upon the world to accomplish the twofold purpose of the tribulation is enormous. The nature of the suffering to be experienced by the nation of Israel is examined in chapter seven. We will examine now the suffering which the world at large will experience.

Israel's suffering will come more from activities of the Antichrist, but the world's suffering will come primarily from devastating worldwide events, symbolized in the book of Revelation under the figures of broken seals, blown trumpets, and poured-out vials of wrath. These events will be directed toward the Gentiles, with the nation of Israel probably being spared from them in large part. This is suggested by such a passage as Isaiah 26:20, 21, "Come, my people, enter thou into thy chambers, and shut thy doors about thee: hide thyself as it were for a little moment, until the indignation be overpast. For, behold, the LORD cometh out of his place to punish the inhabitants of the earth for their iniquity." The seals, trumpets, and vials are themselves symbolic and the descriptions given of what they represent also include considerable symbolism. This symbolism is not easy to identify in all details, but the general significance is clear, as the following discussion will show.

1. *The broken seals* (Rev. 5:1 - 8:1)

The first group of devastating events is symbolized by a successive breaking of seals of a scroll. The scroll is taken by Christ from the hand of God, "sitting upon the throne" (Rev. 5:6, 7). As Christ opens the scroll, breaking the seals in turn, the various events transpire. The nature of the events suggests that they begin shortly after the beginning of the tribulation and conclude by the midpoint of the period.

a. The symbolism.   The events set forth by the first four broken seals are symbolized by a series of horses, each of a different color and bearing a rider. The first horse (Rev. 6:1, 2) is white and carries a rider going forth "to conquer." With no outright war being depicted, it is probable that the mission of the rider is to enforce peace in a world characterized by unrest and disturbance. It may be that a major contributing factor to the disturbance will be the startling departure of great numbers of people in the rapture of the church, which will have recently occurred. The second horse (Rev. 6:3, 4) is red and the rider wields a sword, that he might "take peace from the earth." Here war is clearly represented, meaning that a major conflict will break out soon after the efforts of the first rider have ceased. No clue is given as to its extent or duration. The third horse (Rev. 6:5, 6) is black and the rider carries a pair of balances for weighing food. The symbolism is of famine, probably resulting mainly from the preceding devastating war. The fourth horse (Rev. 6:7, 8) is pale (literally, yellowish-green) and the rider is named Death, having power "to kill with sword, and with hunger, and with death, and with the beasts of the earth." This widespread death results no doubt from both the prior war and the famine.

The fifth broken seal (Rev. 6:9-11) is quite different, presenting a picture of saints in heaven "slain for the word of God." Martyrdom is symbolized here. The significance quite clearly is that persecution has accompanied the other events, probably from the beginning of the tribulation period, with large numbers of saints having been killed for their faith.

The sixth broken seal (Rev. 6:12-17) depicts enormous convulsions of nature, which devastate the earth; men everywhere, of both high and low estate, will cry out in terror, "Hide us from the face of him that sitteth on the throne, . . . for the great day of his wrath is come." These upheavals are often interpreted to be symbolic of political revolutions on earth, but they may be intended quite literally, as depicting actual convulsions of nature (see Matt. 24:7).

b. The time involved. It is probable that, with the opening of the sixth seal, the first half of the tribulation is brought to an end. That is, the events symbolized by these six broken seals take place in the first three and one-half years of the total seven. This is evidenced by the following.

First, events of greatly increased suffering follow these broken-seal events. Several considerations bear out this conclusion. (1) The text (Rev. 6:17) refers to people crying, as a result of the broken sixth seal, that God's great day of wrath is now at hand. (2) The punishments symbolized by the blown trumpets and outpoured vials are described in ensuing chapters of Revelation as being more severe than those of the broken seals. (3) The first verses of the next chapter in Revelation (7:1-3) speak of "the four winds of the earth" being restrained by angels until 144,000 people can be sealed for protection from them; these winds represent the impending great judgments of the blown trumpets and the outpoured vials. The implication is that what is about to come is measurably more severe than what has happened. (4) The opening of the seventh seal, from which the blown trumpets emerge, is followed by a marked silence of one-half hour (Rev. 8:1), suggesting an awesome, foreboding sense of fear in view of what is about to happen.

Second, according to Matthew 24:15-21, this marked increase in suffering comes immediately after the setting up of "the abomination of desolation, spoken of by Daniel the prophet"; this occurs, according to Daniel 9:27, at the midpoint of the tribulation.

Third, Israel experiences a parallel marked change at the midpoint of the tribulation. As seen in the prior discussion, at this point the Antichrist shifts from being a staunch friend of Israel to a bitter enemy. Israel's experience, then, is changed from enjoying good times to enduring the very worst.

2. *The blown trumpets*

We come now to consider the first group of these more severe punishments. Note that these occur just after the midpoint of the tribulation week. Seven angels, standing in God's presence, are given seven trumpets. As each in turn sounds his trumpet, the events of punishment transpire. The blowing of the trumpets must follow the breaking of the seals, since they emerge out of the seventh seal (Rev. 8:1, 2). Interpreting the symbolism of the trumpets is more difficult than interpreting the seals, and a greater difference of opinion exists among Bible scholars as a result. Again, however, the general truth is clear. The first four trumpets, like the first four seals, are similar and may be treated together.

When the first trumpet sounds (Rev. 8:7), one-third of the trees and all green grass are burnt up. When the second sounds (Rev. 8:8, 9), one-third of the sea is turned to blood, resulting in the loss of a third of all ships and sea-life. When the third sounds (Rev. 8:10, 11), a great star, named Wormwood, falls and contaminates a third of the rivers. And when the fourth sounds (Rev. 8:12), a third part of the sun, moon, and stars is darkened, lessening by one-third the light given during both day and night. These figures represent enormous destruction here on earth. A sharp difference of opinion exists concerning the nature of the destruction and the identity of the objects destroyed. Some believe that the physical items listed should all be taken symbolically, representing such entities as human government, the Roman empire, apostate religion, leading persons of the tribulation, etc. It seems wise, however, to understand them literally, to the extent that this can be done reasonably.

Let us move on to consider the last three trumpets. These clearly involve suffering still more severe in nature; the sufferings revealed as the trumpets sound are described as "woes." The first of these woes (fifth trumpet, Rev. 9:1-12) concerns a horde of creatures called "locusts," which bring terrible torment on men generally, except those who have "the seal of God in their foreheads," namely the 144,000 (Rev. 7:3, 4). Since they emerge from the "bottomless pit" (literally, "shaft of the abyss"), they probably represent demons under the control of Satan. The second woe (sixth trumpet, Rev. 9:13-19) involves an army of 200,000,000 horsemen, who kill a third part of men. Since the weapons of this vast army are fire, smoke, and brimstone (Rev. 9:17), which are the weapons of Satan, this group may also be comprised of demons. Note a contrast between these two judgments: whereas the first imparts only severe torment, serious as that may be, the second brings death. The third woe (seventh trumpet, Rev. 11:15-19), which is recorded only after the intervening description of several other matters (Rev. 10:1 - 11:13), concerns, quite in contrast to the first two, the establishment of Christ's millennial kingdom. This one qualifies as a "woe" judgment, parallel to the first two, because it implies the destruction of powers hostile to the program of God, particularly as headed up in the Antichrist. Because this seventh trumpet represents the establishment of the kingdom, it is evident that the seven trumpets together symbolize events spanning the entire second half of the tribulation week.

3. *The poured-out vials of wrath*

Because the trumpet judgments do continue over the last three-and-a-half years of the period, a question arises as to when the last set of judgments falls. One answer suggested is that the vial judgments run contemporaneously with the trumpet judgments and represent basically the same forms of punishment. Support for this view is found in certain striking resemblances which exist between the respective trumpets and vials. One of the difficulties with this view, however, is that Revelation 15:1 speaks of the vials as representing the "seven *last* plagues"; and, also, distinct differences, as well as the similarities, are to be found between the two sets of judgments. A better view, then, is to think of the vial judgments as occurring in a comparatively short period of time, at the very last of the overall period. They would follow most of the trumpet judgments, then, but not all of them, for at least the last trumpet judgment, concerning the establishment of the kingdom, comes a little after the exact close of the tribulation week.

a. Similarities and differences. The following similarities exist between the two sets of judgments. The first four judgments of each set concern the same aspects of the universe: the first with the earth (Rev. 8:7; 16:2), the second with the sea (Rev. 8:8, 9; 16:3), the third with rivers (Rev. 8:10, 11; 16:4-7), and the fourth with outer space (Rev. 8:12; 16:8, 9). Then the sixth judgment of each set mentions the Euphrates River in connection with destructive forces (Rev. 9:13-19; 16:12-16). The seventh judgment makes a clear reference to the close of the seven-year period.

There are marked differences, as well, not only in many detailed aspects of the corresponding judgments, but also in two important general areas. First, the two sets of judgments have contrasting basic characterizations. The trumpet judgments are publicly proclaimed by the blowing of the trumpets, thus stressing the universality of their effect. The vial judgments, being sent forth by the pouring out of the vials of the wrath of God, are presented as punishments distinctly designed by God. Second, the vial judgments, in distinction from the trumpet judgments, are similar to the Egyptian plagues. They are called by the same term (Rev. 15:1, 6) and even show some parallels in the types of plagues involved.

b. The seven vial judgments. The poured-out contents of the first vial of wrath (Rev. 16:2) result in terrible sores breaking out on followers of the Antichrist (thus corresponding to the sixth plague, Exod. 9:8-12). These sores seem to last until at least the time of the fifth vial judgment (Rev. 16:11). The contents of the second vial (Rev. 16:3) render the sea lifeless, so that it is "as the blood of a dead man" (corresponding to the first plague, Exod. 7:20, 21). The contents of the third vial (Rev. 16:4-7) change the rivers into blood, making it necessary for persons who had "shed the blood of saints and prophets" to drink blood (also corresponding to the first plague). The contents of the fourth vial (Rev. 16:8, 9) impart power to the sun to bring widespread death by excessive heat. The contents of the fifth vial (Rev. 16:10, 11) bring darkness on the kingdom of "the beast," i.e., the Antichrist (thus corresponding to the ninth plague, Exod. 10:21-23); this judgment apparently anticipates the complete destruction soon to come at the hand of Christ. The contents of the sixth vial (Rev. 16:12-16) cause the Euphrates River to become dry and "three unclean spirits like frogs" (corresponding to the second plague, Exod. 8:1-6) to emerge from the mouths respectively of "the dragon" (Satan), "the beast" (the Antichrist), and "the false prophet" (the Antichrist's religious partner). These three spirits gather the earthly kings to battle at Armageddon. The contents of the seventh vial (Rev. 16:17-21) bring about mighty convulsions in nature, namely thunders, lightnings, and earthquakes of great intensity, which fully overthrow the ordered affairs of men and bring the tribulation week to a close.

As with the prior two sets of judgments, expositors differ regarding the extent and meaning of the symbolism involved here. Once again, however, whatever the view on details, it is clear that the punishments represented are extremely severe. No question exists but that, because of them, the world will experience suffering of the very worst kind, with the severity increasing as the successive events occur. Note also that, because these last seven judgments are concentrated in the final few weeks or months of the seven-year period, and since they are more severe than even the trumpet judgments, the intensity of suffering during these final weeks or months will be very great indeed.

E. False and True Religion

At the same time that these three sets of judgments take place, there is a significant development in both false and true religion. On the one hand, an apostate church grows and assumes a high position of power; and, on the other, a substantial number of people, commonly called tribulation saints, exercise personal faith in Christ for salvation. Little relation exists between the two groups, so far as their respective development is concerned, but, before many weeks of the tribulation elapse, the first and more powerful group severely persecutes the second.

1. *The apostate church*

Even if an apostate church were not described in the Scripture, as existing during the tribulation week, one might guess that it would be present. An apostate church exists today, already; its members will, of course, not be included in the rapture of the true church. With the true church gone, it will be the only so-called church remaining, and no reason exists for thinking it will disband. Quite the contrary, because it is man's nature to be religious, it could be expected to claim wide allegiance and to assert itself in world power. This is the way the Scriptures present it. The church has always known apostate groups, but in recent years, with the rise of modernism, the extent of apostasy has grown. Aiding in this growth has been what is called the ecumenical movement, which has urged the uniting of various denominations into federated churches. Each time such a union has been formed, a compromise of viewpoint has been required, and this has resulted in a greater overall defection from the truth. All this has brought a very large apostate group into existence today which will continue into the tribulation period.

a. Symbolized as a harlot and as Babylon. The book of Revelation speaks at length of this religious group, especially in chapter 17 and 18, using the figure of a harlot and the name "Babylon." That the intended reference is to the apostate church is evident from several factors. First, the figure of an unfaithful woman fits for the apostate church because the true church is often likened in the New Testament to a bride (see Rom. 7:4; 2 Cor. 11:2; Eph. 5:25-33; Rev. 19:7, 8). The true church is thus a faithful bride and the apostate church an unfaithful one. Second, there is an evident contrast intended between the woman set forth in Revelation 17 with the one in Revelation 12; the latter is properly identified as Israel. Because the Old Testament uses the figure of a wife in respect to Israel, this again makes fitting the contrasting figure of an unfaithful wife for the woman of Revelation 17.

Third, the name Babylon links this person with the city of Rome, for the term Babylon almost certainly was used figuratively for Rome already in early church times. Babylon and Rome were particularly strong and dominant cities in their respective periods and both oppressed the people of God. It may be added that Revelation 17:18 even states directly that this woman is "that great city," meaning Rome.

Fourth, this woman cannot be Rome as a political entity, however, for she rides a "beast" in Revelation 17, and, according to Revelation 13:1-10, this beast symbolizes political Rome. She is no doubt ecclesiastical Rome, that is, Rome as the geographical headquarters of the apostate church. The figure of the woman riding the beast shows political Rome supporting the apostate church, and the church greatly influencing the course of political Rome. Another reason the woman could not be political Rome is because eventually the ten kings of political Rome come to kill her (Rev. 17:16).

b. Significance of this symbolism in Revelation. In view of the above, the significance of the apostate church being symbolized as a harlot becomes apparent — namely to denote the perversion this group makes of the purpose of the true church. Posing as the continuation of the church, now raptured, she will pervert what the true church stood for. One aspect of this perversion may be safely conjectured to be the continued denial of cardinal doctrines set forth in the Bible, such as the inerrant inspiration of the Scriptures, the reality of miracles, the deity of Christ, and the necessity of regeneration for sinful man. Another aspect is definitely symbolized by her committing "fornication" with "the kings of the earth" (Rev. 17:2); this means she will cater to and serve political powers, no doubt to further her own position of strength. Since this form of perversion will involve "kings" (plural) we can assume that these actions will take on widespread proportions. The verse goes on to say that she will make the world's inhabitants drunk with her fornication. This indicates that she will be able to deceive people at large, making them insensible

to her perversions. This deception will be aided by her great influence with the leading powers. Still a third aspect is symbolized
by the fact that she, as a harlot, is called "the mother of harlots"
(Rev. 17:5). The thought is that she will spawn subordinate
church unions, like herself, in various portions of the world. This
will probably be for the purpose of making her own top position
stronger.

The significance of the apostate church being called by the
name Babylon is to show her relation to Rome. During the tribulation period, as will be discussed at greater length in chapter
six, Rome takes on central importance in the world, as the
capital of the restored Roman confederacy. The head of this
restored political entity will be a powerful ruler, depicted in Daniel
7 as a "little horn," and in Revelation 13, as "the beast," who is
properly called the Antichrist. The apostate church, recognizing
the importance of Rome, will seek to enhance her own position
of power by making it her center of operation. Since Rome has
long been the headquarters for Roman Catholicism, it is probable
that there will be, or already will have been, a union formed
between the two religious groups. It is well known that, even in
the present day, there are significant developments in this area.
With such a union between the apostate Protestant church and
the apostate Catholic church, the size and influence of this truly
world church will be very great. This is, no doubt, why political
Rome will be interested in establishing a formal relationship between itself and this powerful organization. The Antichrist, as
he seeks greater power for himself, will be glad to receive all the
support this organization can give; and, at the same time, the
church group will be pleased to enjoy the added strength he can
provide.

c. Reference of Babylon remains the same. There is adequate
reason for believing that the reference of the name Babylon to
ecclesiastical Rome remains the same, whenever it is used in the
book of Revelation. There is a point in noting this, because
some expositors believe that it changes from designating ecclesiastical Rome in Revelation 17 to political Rome especially in
Revelation 18.[5] Their reasoning seems to be that "Babylon" is

---

[5] See, for example, Rene Pache, *The Return of Jesus Christ,* pp. 217-247;
John F. Walvoord, *The Revelation of Jesus Christ,* pp. 258f.

identified definitely with "that great city" in Revelation 18:10, and this is thought to be more in keeping with the idea of political Rome. But "the woman" of Revelation 17 is also definitely called "that great city" (v. 18). Several factors may be listed as evidence for the reference always remaining the same. These concern similarities in the context when the term Babylon is mentioned (Rev. 14:8; 16:19; 17:5; 18:2, 10, 21).

First, the fact that the same term is used in these chapters suggests an identical reference. If it were otherwise, one could expect an indication of the intended change, but this is not found. Second, a similar charge of fornication is made against Babylon in three of the four general passages (14:8; 17:1-5; 18:3, 9). Third, the wrath of God, under the term "wine of wrath," is associated with her in all four of the passages (14:8; 16:19; 17: 16, 17 [implied]; 18:3). Fourth, a similar phrase is used for announcing the destruction of Babylon in two of the passages (14:8 and 18:2): "Babylon (the great) is fallen, is fallen." This is commonly believed to be quoted from Isaiah 21:9. Fifth, a similar description is used for the clothing worn by Babylon in two passages (17:4 and 18:16). That description is: "Purple and scarlet, and decked with gold and precious stones and pearls." Sixth, in two passages (17:16 and 18:8) Babylon is said to be burned with fire. Seventh, in two other passages (17:6 and 18: 24) she is described as having shed the blood of saints in persecution. Such an impressive number of similarities make the identity of the reference in all the passages very likely.

d. The cessation of the apostate church. Since the references to Babylon remain constant, any of the "Babylon" passages may be used for information about the apostate church. The church clearly ceases to exist near the close of the seven-year period. Revelation 16:9, describing the results of the seventh and last vial of wrath, speaks of "great Babylon" receiving the "wine of the fierceness of his [God's] wrath." We have shown previously that the seventh vial is poured out at the end of the tribulation week. Also, the fact that the detailed description regarding her is given after all three sets of judgments have been described, suggests the same time for her demise. At the close of chapter 17, in fact, her demise is described, and, further, chapter 18 tells of the general announcement concerning it. It is probable that, by this time, the Antichrist will see no advantage in the continuing relationship. He will have reached a zenith of power by then and will have no more need of help. Accordingly, he will issue an order, perhaps even making the church illegal and slaying her leaders, and the apostate church will be no more. Since the destruction will come so late in the seven-year period, the Antichrist will not have many days to rule without this ecclesiastical entanglement, but at the time, of course, he will have no way of knowing this.

It should be added that the person called the "false prophet" (Rev. 16:13; 19:20; 20:10), who is best identified as an ecclesiastical head, serving as assistant to the Antichrist, apparently will sever his relation with the apostate church. This follows from the fact that he will not die at the time the church ceases, but will continue to live as long as the Antichrist (Rev. 19:20). If he is the leader of the apostate church earlier, as commonly believed, he evidently will be clever enough to side with the Antichrist against the church in sufficient time to spare his own life. It may be, too, that he will be considered of such great value by the Antichrist (see Rev. 13:12-17; 19:20), for his prior work, that the Antichrist himself will want to maintain a relationship with him, while breaking with the church itself.

2. *Persecution of tribulation saints*

As noted previously, another religious group will exist during the tribulation period. It will be comprised of persons commonly called "tribulation saints"; upon these the apostate church will bring severe persecution.

a. The existence of this group. The existence of this group is established especially by Revelation 7:9-17. The group is there described as "a great multitude, which no man could number," standing before the throne of God (v. 9), having come "out of great tribulation," with robes washed "white in the blood of the Lamb" (v. 14). The implication is that these people have died as martyrs during the tribulation, and that now their tears, resulting from the suffering, are being wiped from their eyes (v. 17). These are Gentiles, since they are distinguished in the context from another group which is definitely composed of Jews (Rev. 7:4-8). This is made clear, also, by the statement that they come from "all nations, and kindreds, and people, and tongues" (v. 9). Note further that the martyrdom occurs in the first half of the tribulation week, because this description in Revelation 7:9-17 is given between the opening of the sixth and seventh seals (cf.

Rev. 6:12 and 8:1). In fact, evidence exists that considerable martyrdom will have occurred up to the time represented by the fifth seal. When this seal is opened, a host is seen in heaven "slain for the word of God" (Rev. 6:9-11).

Three points regarding this group of saints call for special consideration.

The first concerns the manner in which these people will be informed about the Gospel, that they might become saints of God. Who will be witnesses to tell them, when the church has already been raptured to heaven? Sometimes the answer is given that the first to turn to Christ will be those who heard the way of salvation prior to the rapture. This answer is not likely, however, in view of Second Thessalonians 2:10-12. In this passage, Paul states that those who do not receive the truth during this present age will be deceived by the Antichrist, because the Antichrist will have power to perform "signs and lying wonders" as credentials, and because God "shall send them strong delusion that they should believe a lie." The apostle thus warns people against thinking of the tribulation period as a sort of "second chance" for being saved. Those who have thought they would take their chance in not accepting Christ, when the opportunity was theirs during this age, will be deluded into believing in the Antichrist instead. When Paul says this, however, he may have in mind only those persons who have definitely rejected Christ. If so, this would leave the possibility open that any who have heard, but never with sufficient seriousness to have really rejected God's offer, can be saved at that time. These may constitute one source of information for others. The principal source, however, will probably be Bibles, religious books, and tracts, which will still be here in the world. From reading these, people will be able to learn of the Gospel and be prompted to place their trust in Christ.

A second matter concerns the manner of salvation of people, when the Holy Spirit has been "taken out of the way" (2 Thess. 2:7) at the time of the rapture. The Scriptures state clearly that the work of the Holy Spirit is necessary, in this present age, for the imparting of new life in salvation. If He is "taken out of the way" prior to the tribulation, how can people be saved? The answer involves the meaning of the phrase, "taken out of the way." The phrase does not mean that the Holy Spirit will be taken completely out of the world. Actually this would be impossible, for the Holy Spirit is omnipresent. The phrase means only that He will cease one aspect of His work, namely, the restraint of sin in the world. He will not cease all His activity, including the impartation of new life to those who trust Christ as their Savior.

The third matter concerns the large number of people who will be saved during the tribulation period. How can one account for this, when wickedness will reign as never before? The number will indeed be large, for Revelation 7:9-17 discusses only those of the tribulation saints who have been martyred, and they alone are said to be a "great multitude." Two principal matters may be noted in answer. First, the rapture will have occurred, which certainly will have brought great psychological shock to millions of people. They will have experienced the sudden departure from the world of their finest friends and relatives. This will force them to think seriously of religious matters, in a way they have never before desired or thought necessary. Second, there will be a marked increase of sinful activity in the world, over anything known before (2 Thess. 2:6-8), and this will likely be repugnant, especially at first, to a significant number of people. Reacting against it, many will be led to a source of refuge from it, as found in Jesus Christ.

b. The persecution of tribulation saints. This large group of people, truly exercising faith in Christ, will suffer intense persecution at the hands of the apostate church. This is evidenced not only by the existence of so many martyrs in heaven, as early as the midpoint of the tribulation, but by direct statements in Revelation 17:6 and 18:24. In 17:6, the woman riding on the beast is seen to be "drunken with the blood of the saints, and with the blood of the martyrs of Jesus." In 18:24, the statement is made that in the apostate church "was found the blood of prophets, and of saints, and of all that were slain upon the earth." In this terrible activity, of course, the apostate church will have the support, if not the insistence, of the Antichrist, who elsewhere is also described as bringing severe persecution on God's saints (Rev. 13:7; cf. Dan. 7:25). Thousands apparently will have their lives taken, and thousands of others will be made to suffer in horrible ways. The lot of the tribulation saints will not be easy.

Questions for Review

1. List the four classic scripture references which speak of the tribulation as being more severe in suffering than any other time in history.
2. What twofold reference does the term "day of the LORD" often have in the Old Testament?
3. To what two aspects of last-day events does the term "day of the LORD" primarily have reference?
4. What two purposes will the tribulation period serve?
5. Were the Jews familiar with the idea of sevens of years? Explain.
6. At what point in history were the first sixty-nine weeks of Daniel's third vision completed?
7. List the reasons for believing that a long time gap must be placed between the first sixty-nine and the seventieth of Daniel's weeks.
8. Into what two divisions does Daniel 9:27 divide the seventieth week?
9. What does Isaiah 26:20, 21 teach regarding Israel's experience during the tribulation week?
10. What is the likely symbolic meaning of each of the six broken seals of Revelation 6:1-17?
11. Summarize the evidence that these seals will be broken during the first half of the tribulation week.
12. What developments come as each of the first four trumpets sound?
13. What is there about developments from the last three trumpets which calls for them to be characterized as "woes"?
14. Relate the vials of wrath to the trumpets, in respect to the time during the tribulation week when they will be poured out.
15. Identify two general differences between the trumpet judgments and the vial judgments.
16. What developments come as each of the seven vials of wrath are poured out?
17. Under what two figures is the apostate church depicted in Revelation 17 and 18?
18. What is the symbolic significance of these two figures?
19. List reasons for believing that the symbolism of the term "Babylon" in Revelation is always in reference to the apostate church.

20. When and how will the apostate church be brought to an end?
21. What group is designated by the term "tribulation saints"?
22. How will tribulation saints have learned of the Gospel during the tribulation week?
23. In the light of Second Thessalonians 2:7, what can be said as to the work of the Holy Spirit in respect to the salvation of these saints?
24. Give scriptural evidence that these saints will experience severe persecution during the tribulation week.

5

The Church
Spared
From the
Tribulation

In chapter three, the rapture of the church was discussed on the basis that it would precede the tribulation period. As explained in chapter two, this is the position of pretribulationists. They believe that the rapture will precede both the tribulation and the millennium. The most common view held by premillennialists who oppose this position is called posttribulationism. According to this view, the rapture will occur at the close of the tribulation, the church being caught up to meet Christ in the air and then returning with Him immediately to establish the millennial reign. Pretribulationists, then, see the church avoiding the suffering of the tribulation time, while posttribulationists see it going through that period, though being spared from much of the suffering, as will appear in the following discussion. Since the difference is highly significant for every believer, there is good reason to look at the evidence in as much detail as the present chapter will allow. The argumentation below intends to show that the pretribulationist view is the view of Scripture. [1]

A. The Idea of the Tribulation

A few reasons for the church not experiencing the tribulation exist in the very idea of the tribulation. That is, the church's presence

---

[1] For an enlargement of these arguments, see Leon J. Wood, *Is the Rapture Next?*

on earth is not in keeping with the nature and purpose of the tribulation.

1. *The church's presence is not in keeping with the purpose of the tribulation*

The twofold purpose of the tribulation is to punish the Gentile world for its sinfulness through past ages and to bring the nation of Israel to a frame of mind for receiving Christ as the Messiah-Deliverer. The church does not fit into this purpose in either respect, so that the absence of the church from the world would in no way hinder either goal being accomplished. Also, the punishment of the members of the church has been fully met by Christ on Calvary. Though suffering is often permitted by God in the lives of Christians, for the purpose of bringing discipline while on earth, this is something quite different from being made to endure seven years of trial designed especially as worldwide punishment.

2. *The church's presence is not in keeping with the Jewish character of the tribulation*

The tribulation period carries a distinct, special reference to the Jews. That is, the Scriptures present the Jews as playing a quite different role during this period than they do today, while the church is on earth. During the present church age, Jews are viewed as persons to be evangelized and brought into the church as members. Several factors, however, show them to be a distinct group in the tribulation, separate from any Gentile assembly.

Notice first that one of the reasons for the tribulation is to prepare Jews for the revelation of the Messiah as observed above. If the Jews carry this much distinctness during the period, they must be considered by God to have a significance different than in the present age.

A second factor is found in the identification of the tribulation period with the "seventieth week" of Daniel 9, as noted in the prior chapter. It was observed that all prior sixty-nine weeks were related to the history of Israel as a nation, coming to completion with the first appearance of Christ. It is logical then to see the last week as being similarly related to the Jews.

A third factor is seen in a few significant details of Jewish character which are set forth in the descriptions of the period. For instance, Matthew 24:20, in a context describing features of the tribulation, makes reference to the Jewish concept, "sabbath." Also, Revelation 7:2-8 speaks of a group of 144,000 Jews as playing a prominent role during the tribulation week. This group is further identified as composed of persons from all twelve tribes, 12,000 to a tribe.

A fourth factor may be taken from a distinction made during the tribulation between this group of 144,000 Jews and a Gentile host, said to come from "all nations, and kindreds, and people, and tongues" (Rev. 7:9). Both groups are composed of saved people; several statements in Revelation 14:1-5 make this clear regarding the first group; Revelation 7:9-17 identifies the second group as such. But such a distinction between saved Jews and Gentiles is quite foreign to the present age. Today, saved Jews and Gentiles become members of one body, the church (see Gal. 3:28); if the church were present in the tribulation week, one would expect the same to be true then.

3. *Revelation 3:10*

Many posttribulationists agree with pretribulationists that Revelation 3:10 refers to the tribulation period. They disagree, however, on its interpretation. The verse reads, "Because thou hast kept the word of my patience, I also will keep thee from the hour of temptation, which shall come upon all the world, to try them that dwell upon the earth." These words were written to the church at Philadelphia, representing the true and faithful church in the world. Pretribulationists believe the significance of these words to be that the true church will be kept from going through the "hour of temptation" mentioned, a reference to the tribulation. Posttribulationists, on the other hand, see the words to mean that the church will be kept from great suffering during that period, though being present on earth. The following points favor the pretribulationist view.

a. The preposition "from." The use of the preposition translated "from" (Greek, *ek*), in the phrase, "from the hour of temptation," favors it. The meaning of the preposition, used more than 800 times in the New Testament, is "from out of, out from, forth from, from." [2] Its use here calls for the meaning that the church will be taken "out from" the "hour of temptation." The assertion of posttribulationists is that the preposition can mean "from" merely in the sense of non-participation; they say here it could mean the church is to be kept from participating extensively in the suffering of the period.

---

[2] See any standard Greek lexicon.

Support is sought by posttribulationists in John 17:15, where Jesus prays that His disciples may be kept "from the evil." They argue that, because being kept "from the evil" is not accomplished by being taken away from its presence, but only by non-participation, Revelation 3:10 could mean merely that the church will be kept from tribulation suffering in the same way. This conclusion does not follow, however, for the two passages are different. A person can be kept from evil by non-participation, but not from an "hour of temptation." The one is an activity, the other a period of time. A person is either in a period of time, or out of it. If the writer of Revelation had wished to express the idea of preservation within a period of time for the church, he could have used such a preposition as "during," or "through," or "in," but not "from."

b. *Tribulation saints are not spared from suffering.* Even if the posttribulational interpretation of "from" in this passage could be made to stand, the view concerning saints of the tribulation not participating in the suffering of this period cannot be sustained. It should be understood that posttribulationists believe that when "saints" are mentioned in Revelation, these instances are references to the church. Pretribulationists, on the other hand, as indicated in the prior chapter, view them as references to tribulation saints, those saved during the tribulation following the rapture of the church. Numerous passages, which mention these saints, show them to suffer extensively during the tribulation.

For instance, Revelation 13:7 states, "It was given unto him [the beast, Antichrist] to make war with the saints, and to overcome them." Again, a later verse says the Antichrist would "cause that as many as would not worship the image of the beast should be killed" (Rev. 13:15). Further, as noted in the previous chapter, the apostate church is said to be ''drunken with the blood of the saints, and with the blood of the martyrs of Jesus" (Rev. 17:6). In her will be "found the blood of prophets, and of saints, and of all that were slain upon the earth" (Rev. 18:24). Besides these references to martyrdom, there are indications that people will be forced to have "a mark in their right hand, or in their foreheads" in order to "buy and sell" during this period (Rev. 13:16, 17; 19:20). Saints, of course, will refuse such a mark, which would identify them as followers of the Antichrist, and will suffer great deprivation as a result. All this means very great suffering for saints of the day.

It should be said, in fairness, that posttribulationists, in speaking of non-participation in suffering, have in mind primarily the suffering inflicted by God, rather than by men. That is, they see the saints being spared in large part from the sufferings of the "seals," "trumpets," and "vials of wrath." They may be correct in this in some measure (see Rev. 16:2), though the extent is problematical. Apart from this aspect of suffering, however, the pain inflicted by men will be enough to make the time without parallel in past history.

B. Passages Which Imply Imminency of the Rapture

Several passages in the New Testament imply that the rapture of the church is near, because they urge the Christian either to watch for, or exercise hope in view of, the imminent return of Christ. These passages are predicated on the assumption that His return could be at any time. This contradicts the posttribulationists view, which believes that only the tribulation period is imminent, not Christ's coming. Posttribulationists believe that the tribulation could start at any time, but that Christ will come only at the conclusion of that period.

Passages which advocate "watching" for Christ's return will be noted first.

1. The "watching" passages

A number of "watching" passages might be cited, but three will suffice. The first is Romans 13:11, 12, where Paul writes: "For now is our salvation nearer than when we believed. The night is far spent, the day is at hand; let us therefore cast off the works of darkness, and let us put on the armour of light." The word "salvation" refers to the heaven-going of the Christian, in other words, the rapture, when Christians will be delivered from this present evil world. Paul states that this occasion is drawing ever nearer, therefore Christians should cease their "works of darkness" and become occupied instead with the "armour of light." He uses the figure of night drawing to a close, with the following day about to break. The night clearly symbolizes what the Christian experiences in the present evil world, and the day symbolizes deliverance from the world at the rapture. The point made is that the Christian should give attention to a change in life-pattern without delay, because this "salvation" might be brought about at any moment. In other words, Christ could come at any time. The fact that Paul symbolizes the imminent event by a "day" shows that it is to be a happy occasion, such as the rapture, and not sorrowful, such as the tribulation period.

The second passage is First Thessalonians 5:6-8: "Therefore let us not sleep, as do others; but let us watch and be sober. . . . Let us, who are of the day, be sober, putting on the breastplate of faith and love; and for an helmet, the hope of salvation." Here Paul speaks to Christians, "who are of the day," in contrast to the lost, who are "of the night" (v. 5). Paul says that the saved should be alert and watch lest the "day of the Lord" catch them unprepared. The "day of the Lord" means here the tribulation period, described as a time of "sudden destruction" (vv. 2, 3). In verse 9, Paul states that the Christian should watch, because God has appointed him to "salvation" (rapture from this time of wrath) and not to experience the wrath. The Christian's watching, then, is in view of deliverance before the tribulation wrath; this will come, as does the wrath itself, unexpectedly, "as a thief in the night" (v. 2). [3]

The third passage is Luke 12:35-40, [4] which gives two significant illustrations of the importance of watching. The first is of servants who are expected to watch for the return of their master from a wedding. If they are alert to open the door to him immediately on his return, they will be rewarded. The central thought concerns the need for continual watching by the servants that they might be ready to open the door quickly. The second illustration is of "the goodman of the house" who was lax in watching for the thief and, therefore, "suffered his house to be broken through." The point is that the thief comes without prior announcement, making necessary a constant watch by any householder. The passage closes with the appropriate admonition: "Be ye therefore ready also: for the Son of man cometh at an hour when ye think not."

These passages fit the pretribulationist view very well, but not the posttribulationist. According to the former, Christ comes prior to the tribulation, when there will be no advance signs of warning. To be ready for that coming means to be ready all the time, as for a thief in the night. According to the posttribulationists, however, Christ comes after the tribulation and this allows for that seven-year period itself to be just such an advance notice,

---

[3] See pp. 85, 86 for more extensive discussion of this passage.
[4] See chapter 3, pp. 47, 48, for other discussion.

something these passages indicate will not exist. On this basis, seven years after the tribulation begins, or three and one-half years after its midpoint, Christ would come. This means that every person, who hears the witness of tribulation saints (and since the saints will be many in number, this group could be quite sizable and certainly would use effective information of this kind in an effort to be persuasive) will be able to calculate the exact number of months yet remaining before Christ would come.

2. The "hoping" passages

The concept of hope is stressed in the New Testament, and several passages might be brought into the discussion. Two, however, are particularly significant. The first is Titus 2:13, which reads, "Looking for that blessed hope, and the glorious appearing of the great God and our Saviour Jesus Christ." The verse defines the "blessed hope" for which Christians are urged to look as "the glorious appearing of . . . Christ." The Christian is to keep this "blessed hope" prominent in his mind as he plans and conducts his life. The implication is that this "hope" will give him motivation for carrying out the things which Paul has admonished him to do in the preceding verses of the chapter. This "hope," then, is one which may be anticipated with delight, as a truly "blessed" experience. For the pretribulationist, the coming of Christ at the rapture can be joyfully anticipated, for it will bring wonderful deliverance from suffering, earth's limitations, and the presence of sin. For the posttribulationist, however, this is true to a much lesser extent; for according to his view, the Christian will have to face the suffering of the tribulation period before he can expect "the glorious appearing." Christ's coming would still be a blessed experience, but one's delight in anticipating it would be significantly dimmed by the necessary intervening period of trouble. Paul's manner of writing is simply not in keeping with this.

The second passage is James 5:7, 8: "Be patient therefore, brethren, unto the coming of the Lord. . . . Be ye also patient; stablish your hearts: for the coming of the Lord draweth nigh." Once again, the thought set forth is out of keeping with the idea of any factor, like the tribulation, clouding the hope of Christ's coming. The context shows James urging his readers to have patience in the midst of their present suffering and giving them reason to endure it victoriously. The severity of their suffering is suggested by James' comparing it to the affliction suffered by the prophets, who nonetheless, endured patiently (v. 10). James wanted his readers to endure in the same way, by anticipating the deliverance Christ would soon bring.

Once more the pretribulational view fits the thought presented. These Christians could look forward to an imminent coming which would deliver them from their suffering at the time. But again the posttribulational view does not fit. If Christ were not to come until after the tribulation period, these people would have to endure its suffering, additional to and greater than what they were experiencing at the time, before they could anticipate this deliverance. If this were the case, James' words could even have affected them adversely. They might have responded that they hoped Christ's coming would not be in the near future, or even in their lifetime, so that they could avoid the suffering which would precede it.

3. *A counter-argument refuted*

Posttribulationists often counter this type of argument by asserting that the coming of Christ was not considered imminent even in the days of the early church. They support their view with passages which predict events which would occur in the experience of the church; these, it is claimed, delayed Christ's coming until at least those events had taken place. For instance, they point to Christ's farewell address, when the disciples were told that they would suffer persecution (John 15:20; 16:1-3), and that they would perform greater works than they had seen Christ do (John 14:12). Again, during the forty days after the resurrection, Jesus spoke to the disciples about work which they were to do, especially being a witness for Him to all nations (Acts 1:4-8). Also, Paul was told that he would suffer many things for Christ (Acts 9:16; 20:23); he, in turn, told the Ephesian elders that they should beware of "grievous wolves" that would come in among them (Acts 20:29). The item most often mentioned is Jesus telling Peter that he would grow old and die.

a. The generality of the items concerned. In responding to this line of reasoning, it may be noted first that most of these "necessary" events were very general in nature. They did not require any specific length of time to complete. Jesus said that the disciples would suffer persecution, but did not state how much or how long it would last. He said that they would perform great works, but did not specify how many or the length of time needed to effect them. Witnessing to all nations could appear to require more time, but how complete did such coverage need to be? Christ could hardly have meant every tribe and tongue of all time, for some had already arisen in various parts of the world and died out again before He came to earth. Moreover, if He had meant that, His coming has not been possible at any time in history and still is not. Paul's own suffering and his prediction about "grievous wolves" in the Ephesian church are likewise intangibles as far as length of time is concerned.

   b. The item of Peter's growing old and dying. The one item which is more definite in nature concerns Peter's growing old and dying. Jesus' words to Peter were, "When thou wast young, thou girdest thyself, and walkedst whither thou wouldest: but when thou shalt be old, thou shalt stretch forth thy hands, and another shall gird thee, and carry thee whither thou wouldest not" (John 21: 18). The text adds that Jesus was thereby signifying by what death Peter should glorify God. This means, true enough, that Christ could not come until after Peter had died. Note however, that this only proves a definite end to Peter's life, and not a definite length of time; and it is the latter which is necessary for the argument of posttribulationists. For who knew how long Peter would live? Jesus did speak of Peter's growing old, but Peter was no longer young when Jesus spoke. In fact, Jesus used the phrase regarding Peter, "when thou wast young," implying that he was no longer young at the time. This means no one could say, within a very few years following Jesus' statement, that Christ could not come at any time. Peter's death soon became imminent, and Christ's coming became correspondingly imminent.

   c. A conclusion. Some premillennial expositors have asserted that the coming of Christ has been imminent even from Pentecost. This, however, cannot be true, for the church only started then. Christ could hardly come for the church until it had existed for a little time at least. But this amount of time did not have to be extensive. Indeed, by the time the "watching" and "hoping" passages were written, it would seem that it would not have had to extend any longer. By then, the church was well under way, persecution had been suffered, marvelous works had been performed, and the gospel message had been spread far and wide. As for Peter, by the time he penned the words, "But the end of all things is at hand" (1 Pet. 4:7), sufficient years had passed to satisfy Jesus' words about Peter growing old. Peter had to be content with knowing that he would not see that coming himself; but he was quite aware that, even as he could die at any time, so Christ could come at any time, and others would witness that blessed occasion.

C. Passages From First and Second Thessalonians

The Spirit of God inspired Paul to include several significant references to Christ's return in the epistles to the Thessalonian church. For this reason it is appropriate to devote a section to them. Four passages will be discussed.

1. *First Thessalonians 4:13-18*

The first passage is First Thessalonians 4:13-18, which has been discussed at some length in chapter three.[5] It is pertinent to note the passage again, this time particularly to gain evidence in favor of the pretribulational view. The thrust of Paul's words, as noted previously, is that the Thessalonians were anxious concerning those of their number who had died; he wanted to relieve this anxiety by assuring them that "the dead in Christ" would suffer no loss at all. In fact, they would even precede the living in meeting Christ in the air at the rapture.

Pretribulationists and posttribulationists agree on this basic interpretation of the passage. However, posttribulationists face a difficulty. A question arises regarding the logic of the Thessalonians' anxiety. If they believed the coming of Christ would not occur until after the seven-year tribulation, was not their anxiety for the departed dead misplaced? Should they not rather have been concerned about themselves? For, if the tribulation were near at hand, as apparently they believed, they were facing the beginning of severe suffering. Those who had died would at least escape this foreboding time, but those who lived would not. However, the Thessalonians do not show any concern for themselves, but only an anxiety for those who had left them in death.

The pretribulational view, on the other hand, fits very well. On this basis, the Thessalonians were anticipating being caught home to heaven in the rapture, prior to the outbreak of the seven-year suffering, and of course were not concerned for themselves. They wanted to be sure, however, that the departed ones would not miss this glorious occasion because of having died. Paul

---

5See above, pp. 42-44.

assures them that they would not miss it, but would even be raptured in advance of those yet living.

2. *First Thessalonians 5:1-11*

The second passage is First Thessalonians 5:1-11. This immediately follows the one just discussed. The gist of Paul's thought is that "the day of the Lord" will come "as a thief in the night," and will catch people unprepared for it. These people will be thinking in terms of "peace and safety" for themselves, but will experience "sudden destruction" instead. Then he admonishes the Thessalonian Christians that they, being "children of the day," should not be caught similarly by surprise, but should be well prepared by living in a God-pleasing manner. The apostle closes with the joyful note that God has not appointed them to suffer a time of wrath, such as "the day of the Lord," therefore they should comfort one another.

Two points favor the pretribulational position. The first concerns the words, "peace and safety," which the text says will characterize the thinking of people just prior to the coming of "the day of the Lord." That such thinking should be found generally in the world, at the time indicated, fits the pretribulational view very well. On this basis, "the day of the Lord" here refers to the tribulation period; [6] prior to this time of suffering, people will indeed be sufficiently self-confident to be thinking in such terms. The situation is different for the posttribulationist, however, because he takes "the day of the Lord" to refer to the judgment Christ brings following the tribulation. After seven years of tribulation, men will hardly be saying "peace and safety." They will be crying, rather, for help and relief from their terrible plight.

The other concerns the note of comfort in verse 11. This again fits the pretribulation position very well. Paul was extending this comfort to the Thessalonian Christians because they could expect to be delivered from suffering through Christ's pretribulational coming. This suffering would instead fall on those who were now oppressing them and who were so confidently crying "peace and safety." This was reason for comfort, indeed. But with the posttribulational position the deliverance would be from the posttribulational time of wrath which would follow the longer tribu-

---

[6] See chapter 4, pp. 55, 56, for discussion.

lational time of suffering. On this basis, then, Paul would be comforting the Thessalonians in respect to a time of suffering which was several years in the future, while saying nothing about a longer time of suffering which would intervene. It is hard to imagine Paul writing in such a manner.

3. *Second Thessalonians 1:5-10*

The third passage is Second Thessalonians 1:5-10. Paul's concern here is not the rapture of the church but Christ's posttribulational coming, when He brings judgment on "them that know not God." That is why the descriptive terms used concerning the coming are quite different from those noted in the first two passages. For instance, Christ is here said to come "in flaming fire taking vengeance" (v. 8). That which brings Paul to speak of this occasion is again the affliction which the Thessalonian Christians were experiencing. In verse 4, he introduces the subject by speaking of the "patience and faith" of the Thessalonians in the midst of this suffering as a "manifest token" that God would in due time bring judgment on their oppressors. Then he compares the future state of both the oppressors and the Thessalonians, as he says that "it is a righteous thing with God to recompense tribulation to them that trouble you"; but the Thessalonians, in contrast, would enjoy "rest" along with Paul and other saints. The Thessalonians could take comfort, then, in knowing that the time was coming when those who now were making them suffer would experience even worse suffering themselves, and that, when this was true for them, the Thessalonians would be enjoying blessed rest and relief. Paul continues the subject by describing the time of Christ's coming, when this contrasting situation would come true — a time when all enemies of Christ would be dealt with in wrath and when Christ would "come to be glorified in his saints."

Once more, a clear point in favor of the pretribulational view exists. Paul does not mention that tribulational suffering will have to precede this promised time of blessed "rest." According to the posttribulational view, Paul would be extending comfort to these suffering Thessalonians by reminding them that they would be given a "rest" from their present condition, just as soon as Christ would come, while knowing that beforehand still a longer period of suffering would intervene. Again, it is difficult to believe that Paul would write in this manner.

4. *Second Thessalonians 2:1-17*

The fourth and last passage is Second Thessalonians 2:1-17. It is the longest and calls for the most discussion. Paul notes first that the Thessalonians have a troubled mind, due to false instruction by other teachers. They are concerned lest "the day of the Lord" [7] has already come. [8] Paul wants to assure them that this has not happened and gives two reasons by which they may know this. The first is that "a falling away" has not yet occurred, and the second is that the "man of sin" has not been revealed. Paul continues by describing this "man of sin" (the Antichrist) as a very proud person, even exalting himself above God. Then Paul speaks of Him "who now letteth" (the Holy Spirit, who restrains sin) as being "taken out of the way," which will make it possible for this "man of sin" to appear. He will deceive people into believing his lie, resulting in their condemnation; but he will eventually be consumed by the Lord. Paul closes by expressing gratefulness that God has not appointed Christians to this time of tribulational wrath (when the "man of sin" will be active), and by urging the Thessalonians to stand fast in the faith and to comfort one another.

In this passage, no less than four points give evidence in favor of the pretribulational view.

a. *The "falling away."* The first point concerns the word translated "falling away" (v. 3). The Greek word is *apostasia,* coming from the verb *aphistemi,* meaning "to go away, depart." The noun form has been adopted into the English language to mean "a departure from the faith," but it is not at all certain that that is its meaning here. The word is used only one other time in the New Testament (Acts 21:21), and the context there does not concern last things. The thought, rather, is to a "departure" from the teachings of Moses, which Paul was alleged to have advocated. In no instance, then, is it used to mean a departure from the faith in the last days, unless it is here.

Paul simply says that "the day of the Lord" cannot come until the "departure" occurs first. What type of a departure fits

---

[7] See v. 2. The best manuscripts read "the day of the Lord," not "the day of Christ" as in the King James.

[8] The word used (enestēken) is better translated as something already existent, instead of being merely "at hand." It is always translated that way elsewhere in the N.T. (cf. 1 Cor. 7:26; 2 Tim. 3:1; Heb. 9:9).

best into the context? Is it a departure from the faith? In later books, (e.g., 1 Tim. 4:1, 2; 2 Tim. 3:1-9; 4:3, 4), Paul does refer to the last days as a time when men will forsake the faith; but he has made no mention of that idea in either First or Second Thessalonians, and these were the first he wrote. So, then, as the Thessalonians would have read this usage of the word *apostasia,* they would have had no background for understanding it as a departure from the faith. Also, since Paul does not refer to the idea of last-day defection from the faith in any of his books, until the last he wrote, it is not likely that it was a subject of which he spoke orally to churches this early in his ministry. Further, when Paul does present the idea in his last books, he does not employ the word *apostasia* in doing so, [9] which suggests that, even then, Paul did not particularly associate this word with the idea. What thought did he wish to convey when he used it here, then? The answer best suiting all these considerations is a departure of Christians from the earth in the rapture. This was the subject on Paul's mind and on the minds of the Thessalonians, as the opening words of this very passage show (2 Thess. 2:1). This provides most convincing evidence for pretribulationism, because Paul would be stating directly that the rapture will precede the tribulation period.

b. Identity of the "restrainer." Another point concerns the identity of the one who restrains sin in the present world (2:6-8). Pretribulationists believe that this one is the Holy Spirit, who does maintain a curb on sin in the world, as several Scriptures show (see Gen. 6:3; Job 1:10; Isa. 59:19; 63:10, 11; John 16:8). Posttribulationists suggest other possible identities, not agreeing among themselves, for none of the identities really fit. One suggestion is that this restrainer was the Roman empire of ancient time, which, as the governing authority did serve to control lawlessness. If this identification is correct, however, then the Antichrist should have made his appearance at the time of the fall of the empire, for the text says that the wicked one will be revealed when the one that restrains is "taken out of the way." Another suggestion is Satan, but how this prince of darkness can be thought of as one who restrains lawlessness is difficult to follow. Still another is human government in general, which again may be

---

[9] One time only, in First Timothy 4:1, he uses the verbal form *apostesontai,* which is from the same verbal root, *aphistemi.*

said to curb sin. Human government, however, under the leadership of the Antichrist, will continue after the Antichrist begins his work. All these suggestions simply raise too many objections to be acceptable.

This leaves the Holy Spirit as most likely the one Paul meant. Just why Paul did not identify Him by name is not made clear, but apparently he had discussed the general subject with the Thessalonians sufficiently that the descriptive reference was considered adequate. This again favors the pretribulational view. Posttribulationists believe that the church will be on earth during all of the tribulation period, just as in the present age, and this makes any change in the activity of the Holy Spirit during that time quite unlikely. Pretribulationists, however, believing that the church will have been removed by this time, do not have this problem.

c. The "salvation" of verse 13. A third matter concerns the word "salvation" of verse 13. Paul states that God has chosen the Thessalonian Christians "to salvation through sanctification of the Spirit and belief of the truth." Because the apostle has just been speaking about the severe suffering of the tribulation period, the logical, primary reference of this "salvation" is to deliverance from that time. He doubtless has salvation from all punishment in mind secondarily, for "sanctification of the Spirit and belief of the truth" apply to deliverance in the fullest sense. But the general context of the passage suggests that Paul was especially referring to the suffering of the tribulation. Thus Paul is saying that Christians will be spared from the tribulation period.

d. The concepts, "shaken," "troubled," and "comfort." The fourth matter concerns the concepts "shaken" and "troubled" of verse 2 and "comfort" of verse 17. The two words of verse 2 express strong emotional feeling; they indicate that the Thessalonian Christians were seriously disturbed, in view of which Paul voices the note of comfort in verse 17. Posttribulationists suggest that the matter causing this anxiety was the approaching time of wrath, when Christ would come at the close of the tribulation to punish the unbelieving world. They see the Thessalonians believing that they were already in the tribulation, thinking that this "day of the Lord" was then "at hand." If this were the correct interpretation, however, it would seem that, rather than being "shaken" and "troubled" at this prospect, these Christians would have been joyful and full of anticipation. For this would be the time when they would be raptured to meet their Lord, with vengeance being meted out upon their present persecutors? Why would Paul have felt led to extend comfort on such a basis? The Thessalonians would not have needed comfort, but encouragement to wait patiently until that time of deliverance.

Pretribulationists, on the other hand, find that this anxiety of the Thessalonians fits their view very well. These Christians were afraid lest the tribulation period had already started; this meant that they either had missed the rapture or else had misunderstood Paul's previous teaching regarding the time of its occurrence. On either basis they now had to endure seven years of suffering. They probably thought that the suffering they were already experiencing was the beginning of the tribulation and could only believe, then, in view of what Paul had apparently taught them (v. 5), that the days ahead would become still worse. This was indeed reason to be troubled.

D. Other Evidence

Pretribulationists can point to two other areas in their favor. The first and principal one concerns the Olivet Discourse.

1. *The Olivet Discourse*

Posttribulationists frequently use the Olivet Discourse of Christ as a principal source of evidence in favor of their view. When properly understood, however, this discourse agrees with the rest of Scripture in support of pretribulationism, as shown especially by two passages to be discussed. Some analysis of the discourse must first be presented as background. [10]

a. Analysis of the discourse. The discourse is recorded in Matthew 24, 25, Mark 13, and Luke 21. It was delivered by Christ during the last week before the crucifixion, probably on Tuesday evening, shortly after He left the Temple for the last time. Speaking primarily concerning last-day events, Christ sought to answer two questions which had been presented by the disciples. One concerned the time when Christ would come to earth again to establish the Jewish kingdom; the second concerned the nature of the signs which would herald His coming. Jesus answered the two questions by devoting approximately one-half of the discussion to each. Jesus answers the "time" question in Matthew 24:4-31 and 25:31-46; the "sign" question is answered between these two

---

[10] See Wood, *Is the Rapture Next?* pp. 88-105, for greater detail.

sections, from 24:32 to 25:30. In Mark and Luke the division is similar, except that their accounts are less complete and omit entirely the last portion of the "time" division, concerning a judgment scene.

To understand Jesus' meaning, it is important to keep this basic division of the discourse in mind. Posttribulationists fail to do this when they assert that they have a convincing argument against pretribulationism here because there is no mention of the rapture. Actually, one should not expect Jesus to have made a specific reference to the rapture in this context, for He was answering the disciple's question concerning the time when the Jewish kingdom would be established. The rapture concerns the glorification of the church, not the establishment of the Jewish kingdom. At the same time, however, when this division is kept in mind, there is good reason for discerning an implication of the rapture, particularly in the "sign" section. For example, Jesus there urges the disciples to watch diligently for His coming (Matt. 24:42-44). His language is strikingly similar to that noted earlier in passages having a clear reference to the rapture. Because this admonition occurs in the "sign" section, where chronological sequence is not pertinent, one may safely take it as an implied reference to the rapture. This could not be true if it came in the "time" section, for chronological sequence is observed there. The "sign" section, however, does not follow chronological order and can include implications of church-related aspects, as well as direct information concerning Jewish matters.

It was not appropriate for Jesus to speak directly of the rapture at this time, for the disciples were not prepared to understand it. They knew almost nothing about the church since Jesus had not instructed them regarding it as yet. They would learn of it in due time, and that would be the time to become specific. Also, at that time, they would be able to look back and understand what implications had been given earlier, such as here in this discourse. It was enough now to refer directly only to Jewish-related matters, with which they were much concerned and which they were able to understand.

b. Luke 21:28. Two passages especially give evidence that Jesus did have the rapture in mind as He voiced much of this discourse. The first of these reads, "And when these things begin to come to pass, then look up, and lift up your heads; for your redemption draweth nigh" (Luke 21:28). Immediately preceding this verse, Luke mentions the appearing of the Son of Man in glory. This locates the verse in the historical or "time" section of the discourse, where chronological order is followed. In fact it is the last statement in that section, and only Luke records it. It says that "when these things *begin* to come to pass," then Christians should expect their redemption. The word for "begin" (Greek, *archomenōn,* from the root, *archō,* meaning "to be first") is stressed by being placed as the initial word in the sentence. It does not mean that the subject is merely one of a beginning group, but that it is itself the first item. The significance is that the disciples should "look up" and expect their redemption as the first item in the things previously listed. Some expositors take the plural "these things" (Greek, *toutōn*) as referring only to items mentioned beginning with verse 25, but there is no reason for limiting them at this point. Jesus has been listing parallel items from verse 8. All have a direct continuity, for all refer to tribulation events.

The thought, then, is that the disciples should think back before all of these items, before indeed all of the events of the tribulation, as the point at which to expect their "redemption." A paraphrase of the verse appears as follows: "But as the first item in this series of events just listed, look up and lift up your heads, for at that moment your redemption draws near." "Redemption is generally accepted as referring here to the rapture. This is particularly substantiated by such a verse as Romans 8:23.

Jesus' logic in inserting this statement at the end of this list of events is noteworthy. What He has been saying, in listing all of the prior items, is that the tribulation time will be most unpleasant to experience. All the events will involve severe suffering for those on earth. Jesus has closed by noting the coming of the "Son of man . . . with power and great glory"; this occasion, as known from parallel texts, will bring further terrible suffering. Thus, He wishes now to finish with a hopeful note, to give a word of encouragement for those who are His own. Therefore, He mentions the "redemption" which they will receive by His previous coming. This could hardly be the coming which He has just noted, as posttribulationists hold, for it is placed here in contrast to it. That one fits in sequence with all the items of suffering noted, but this one constitutes a "redemption" from those items; this is indicated further by the use in this verse of the adversative *de* ("but"), instead of the continuative *kai* ("and") of the previous verses.

c. Luke 21:36. The second verse which indicates that Jesus had the rapture in mind is Luke 21:36. It reads, "Watch ye therefore, and pray always, that ye may be accounted worthy to escape all these things that shall come to pass, and to stand before the Son of man." In contrast to the other verse, this one occurs in the "sign" section of the discourse. Its place in that section corresponds to Matthew 24:42-44, where Jesus bids the disciples to "watch, therefore; for ye know not what hour your Lord doth come." Here, however, Jesus not only urges the disciples to "watch," but to do so that they might "be counted worthy to escape all these things."

"These things" are best taken to be those of which Jesus has been speaking in the "time" section, concerning the tribulation period. The important word here is "escape" (from the Greek root, *ekpheugō,* meaning, "to flee away, escape"). It means to move away quickly from a situation of danger or unpleasantness (cf. Acts 16:27; 19:16; 2 Cor. 11:33). Thus, Jesus is saying that an attitude of watching and prayer will qualify the Christian to move away quickly from the danger of the tribulation events. Such an escape would have to take place, obviously, prior to the beginning of those events. Some interpreters seek to avoid this natural interpretation by asserting that "escape" need mean only "to stand firm through affliction." This will not do, however, for the verb never carries this idea in the New Testament. [11] Others, more careful in their work, take "these things" as referring only to the events implied in the one phrase of verse 26, "those things which are coming on the earth." [12] In this way, the "escape" in view is limited to those events of affliction (here only implied) which Christ brings at His posttribulational coming. Where they find license for making this limitation is not clear. Certainly, the more natural reference is to all the items Jesus has listed, for all involve severe suffering. Why should He have referred only to matters merely implied when He has listed many others directly?

Both these verses, then, point to the pretribulation rapture idea and show that Jesus did have this concept in mind, by way of implication, especially when He dealt with the "sign" aspect of the discourse. As observed, He did not mention the rapture

---

[11] The verb *ekpheugo* is used 7 times and *pheugo* 31, always with the idea of "flee" or "escape."

[12] See, e.g., G. E. Ladd, *The Blessed Hope,* pp. 86-88.

directly, for the disciples at the time knew little about church-related truth and would not have understood Him. The information was implied, however, for them to note and benefit from, as soon as the church age would begin, when they would be in a position both to understand and profit.

2. *Millennial inhabitants*

The other area of additional evidence for the pretribulational view concerns those who will inhabit the earth during the millennial reign of Christ. Pretribulationists believe those inhabitants will be the living saints who will survive the tribulation period. As seen in the previous chapter, many people will exercise true faith in Christ during the seven-year time. A great host of these will suffer death as martyrs, as also noted, but many others will survive and still live at the close of the time. These will be found righteous by Christ at the time of His judgment of Jews and Gentiles following the tribulation [13] and will be granted the wonderful blessing of entering the thousand-year period.

According to posttribulationists, however, there will only be glorified saints on the earth during Christ's reign. They believe that the rapture of the church, which will include saints of all time, will occur after the tribulation is finished. Being raptured, all the saints will be glorified. These, then, will return with Christ immediately and become earth's inhabitants during Christ's reign. But this would mean that if there are to be any non-glorified people on earth during the millennium, they must be unsaved. This seems out of keeping with the blessing God is said to pour out on the world during this time. Indeed, how could the earth then "be full of the knowledge of the LORD, as the waters cover the sea" (Isa. 11:9)? On the other hand, if one does not allow for this possibility, then the only inhabitants would be glorified saints; and on this basis, one could not account for the presence of sin on earth [14] or for the source of the revolutionary army Satan forms at the close of the millennium (Rev. 20:7-9).

---

[13] See chapter 8, pp. 149-153 for discussion. Probably many believing Jews will enter the millennium directly, without experiencing any time of judgment. All Gentiles, however, will have to be approved before entrance will be given.

[14] See chapter 9, pp. 177, 178 for discussion.

Questions for Review

1. In what way is the church's presence on earth not in keeping with the twofold purpose of the tribulation?
2. What four points indicate that the tribulation period carries a definitely Jewish character?
3. Summarize the evidence from Revelation 3:10 which shows that the church will not be on earth during the tribulation period.
4. What scripture proof may be cited that saints on earth during the tribulation period will experience severe suffering?
5. How do "watching" passages support the pretribulational position?
6. How do "hoping" passages support the pretribulational position?
7. What counterargument is sometimes raised by posttribulationists to the arguments from these passages?
8. How may this counterargument be answered?
9. At what point in church history may one say that the coming of Christ became imminent?
10. What argument for pretribulationism may be taken from 1 Thessalonians 4:13:18?
11. What two points from First Thessalonians 5:1-11 may be cited in favor of pretribulationism?
12. In what way does Second Thessalonians 1:5-10 give evidence in favor of pretribulationism?
13. Review the evidence which shows that the Greek word *apostasia* in Second Thessalonians 2:3 refers to the rapture.
14. Show that the "restrainer" of Second Thessalonians 2:6-8 must be the Holy Spirit.
15. In what way does the word "salvation" in Second Thessalonians 2:13 present an argument in favor of pretribulationism?
16. How do the concepts "shaken," "troubled," and "comfort," in Second Thessalonians 2:2, 17 support pretribulationism?
17. Into what two divisions should the Olivet discourse be divided?
18. Should one expect the concept of the church to be found in the chronological division of the Olivet discourse? Explain.
19. How do Luke 21:28, 36 give evidence in favor of pretribulationism?

6

The
Antichrist

The dominant person in the tribulation period will be the Antichrist. He, as king of a restored form of the Roman empire, will continue to grow in power and influence as the seven years of the period pass. Especially significant is the fact that he will become the principal source of suffering for the nation of Israel during the last half of the period. As has been noted, the people of Israel will probably escape much of the horror brought on the rest of the world by the broken seals, blown trumpets, and poured-out vials, but they will become the prime recipients of the suffering which the Antichrist effects. The Scriptures present him as a fully controlled tool of Satan, used to effect Satan's program for the tribulation; this program will include this time of suffering for God's chosen people Israel. God is willing to permit the suffering so that His people will be brought to a frame of mind for receiving Christ as their Messiah-Deliverer at the climax of the seven-year time. The scriptural portrait of the Antichrist may be obtained by a study of several key passages of Scripture.

A. Scriptural Use of the Term "Antichrist"

Surprisingly, the term "antichrist" appears only five times in the Bible, and all five are in John's first and second epistles. John uses the term twice in First John 2:18, saying, "As ye have heard

that antichrist shall come, even now are there many antichrists";
once in 2:22, "He is antichrist, that denieth the Father and the
Son"; once in 4:3, "And every spirit that confesseth not that Jesus
Christ is come in the flesh is not of God; and this is that spirit
of antichrist, whereof ye have heard that it should come"; and
once in Second John 7, "For many deceivers are entered into the
world, who confess not that Jesus Christ is come in the flesh.
This is a deceiver and an antichrist." Four of the five occurrences
are in reference to people of John's day who were opposed to
Christ and His work, either denying His deity (2:22) or the fact
that He had come in the flesh (4:3, 2 John 7). Only once does
it refer to the person of the future with whom this chapter is
concerned. This is in First John 2:18, "As ye have heard that
antichrist shall come." Even here, however, no information is
given as to whom John had in mind. It seems clear that he did
have a definite person in view, and probably could have described
him at some length had the occasion called for it. But he does not
do so, which means that in no passage of the Bible is a person
bearing this name described. The result is that the identity and
description of the one John had in mind must be discerned from
a study of the various persons who are set forth in apocalyptic
texts.

Before beginning an inquiry as to the identity of the Antichrist, we should determine the meaning of the term "antichrist."
The meaning is twofold in nature. One aspect is implied in John's
use of the term as he speaks of people opposed to Christ. People
of his day were antichrist if they manifested an antagonism to
Christ. The Antichrist of the future, then, will be one who is
similarly opposed to Christ and all for which Christ stands. The
other aspect comes from the basic meaning of the Greek preposition *anti,* which is the prefix used in the name. This basic meaning is "substitute for" or "in place of." This meaning, then, speaks
of the Antichrist as a person who takes the place of Christ, who
substitutes for him. Actually this meaning is the more fundamental
of the two; the antagonism will arise from the substitution because of hostility in attitude. It may be concluded that the person
properly designated as the Antichrist will be one who will both
substitute for Christ and stand opposed to Him.

The particular person in apocalyptic texts who is best identified with this twofold role is one called by three different terms,
each depicting him from a distinct point of view. In Daniel, he is

called the "little horn"; in Revelation, the "beast"; and in Second Thessalonians, the "man of sin."

B. The "Little Horn" of Daniel

Daniel refers to the Antichrist in several passages, two of which are important for study at this point. In the first of these, the characteristic term "little horn" is used, and in the other only the general designation, "king." A third passage calls for attention also, because in it another person, who lived in ancient history, is significantly called by the same term "little horn."

1. Daniel 7

The term "little horn" is used in Daniel 7, where the first of Daniel's four visions is described. This first vision is the most comprehensive in meaning of the four. The other three visions reveal additional information related to aspects of the overall history set forth in this one. The history involved concerns the successive empires of Babylonia, Medo-Persia, Greece, and Rome of ancient time, and then of Rome again, in a restored form, during the tribulation period.

a. The four empires. The history of the four empires is symbolized by four animals, with the fourth one giving birth to the little horn, which is of central interest here. The first animal is a lion, having eagle's wings (v. 4); it represents Babylonia, the empire in power when Daniel had his vision. Two facts show that this is the intended representation. First, the lion as the king of animals and the eagle as the king of birds correspond in significance to the "head of gold" in Nebuchadnezzar's earlier dream (Dan. 2:32, 38). This head of gold is specifically said to represent Nebuchadnezzar, the great king of Babylonia. Second, the information given about this animal fits well with the history of the later years of Nebuchadnezzar's rule. [1]

The second animal is a bear with three ribs in its mouth (v. 5); it represents Medo-Persia. This follows from the fact that Medo-Persia did succeed Babylonia in history. Also, Medo-Persia conquered vast areas of territory, which is symbolized especially by the three ribs in the bear's mouth.

The third animal is a leopard with four wings (v. 6); it represents Greece. The Greek empire succeeded the Medo-Persian

---

[1] See Leon J. Wood, *A Commentary on Daniel,* for discussion.

empire, and did so with great rapidity. The element of rapidity is symbolized by the very nature of the leopard, which is the swiftest of animals, and by the four wings on its back.

The fourth animal is not identified, but is described as exceedingly strong (v. 7); it represents Rome. The Roman empire succeeded Greece, and was noted for its great strength. This resulted in its continuing for a longer time than the other three empires taken together.

b. The restoration of the Roman empire. An item of major significance concerning this fourth animal is that it has ten horns, which are described in verse 24 as symbolizing "ten kings." Since these horns exist at the same time, and since the little horn, soon to be introduced, grows out from among them, the kings so symbolized must reign concurrently. This idea of concurrence is significant because at no time in the history of ancient Rome, for all of its approximately six centuries of existence, did ten contemporaneous kings rule. This fact provides a clue that two different periods of existence are to be distinguished here for the Roman empire. One is the empire of past days, and the other is a Roman empire to be restored. If the empire of past days did not fulfill the predictive history set forth, then there has to be a restoration, for the Scriptures are never inaccurate. This change of reference can most logically be located in the phrase, "and it had ten horns." Thus the beast symbolizes ancient Rome in the text prior to this phrase and future Rome beginning with and following this phrase.

c. The little horn. The little horn of interest in this discussion is introduced in verse 8, where it is said to displace three of the original horns as it grows. This leaves a total of seven. The king represented by the little horn is described as having "the eyes of a man," suggesting keenness of insight, and as having "a mouth speaking great things," indicating that he will be boastful.

This little horn is further described in verses 24-26, in the portion of the chapter devoted to the interpretation of the vision. In verse 24, the ten horns are definitely identified as ten kings, as noted; it is implied that the little horn is also a king. The fact that this one is "diverse from" the others and is able to displace three of them shows that he becomes the leader of the others. In verse 25 he is again depicted as a boaster, even speaking "great words against the most High." The verse states further that he will make "the saints of the most High" to suffer, a characteristic noted earlier regarding the Antichrist. [2] He also will "think to change times and laws," a likely reference to an attempt even to change laws of nature which pertain to time. [3] He will continue in this activity for a period described as "a time and times and the dividing of time."

This last phrase, which is really a formula denoting a period of time, is used again in Daniel 12:7 and Revelation 12:14; in the latter verse it is made parallel with 1,260 days (see Rev. 12:6), or three-and-a-half years. Actually, putting together the singular "time," the plural "times," and a "dividing of time" makes sense only if it does mean three-and-a-half times, or three-and-a-half years. As will be seen in the next chapter, this duration of time corresponds to the last half of the tribulation week, at the beginning of which the Antichrist breaks his covenant with Israel. [4] He will then be at the height of his power during this period, having worked to attain it during the first half of that week of years.

Verse 26 implies that the demise of the little horn will be sudden and complete. This will be discussed in a later chapter.

2. Daniel 8

Before speaking of the second passage in Daniel which presents this same king of the future, it is well to note Daniel 8 which again uses the term "little horn," but of a person of ancient history. This passage also carries significance in reference to the Antichrist.

a. The two empires, Medo-Persia and Greece. This passage sets forth Daniel's second vision. Once again animals are seen, but this time there are only two — a two-horned ram and a one-horned goat. The ram, said in verse 20 to represent Medo-Persia (corresponding, then, to the bear of the first vision), is depicted as making a sweeping conquest of enemies "westward, and northward, and southward," almost without opposition (v. 4).

---

[2] See chapter 4, p. 72. Interestingly, the word translated "wear out" in the text is the same as used regarding the wilderness clothes of the Israelites not wearing out (Deut. 8:4; 29:5; Neh. 9:21).

[3] At the time of the French revolution, an attempt was made to start a ten-day week.

[4] See chapter 7, pp. 118-120.

It had two horns, with the higher of the two coming up last (v. 3). Medo-Persia did conquer extensively under Cyrus the Great and did so with comparative ease. Also, the Persian division of the Medo-Persian empire did rise to power after the Median division, and then became the more important of the two, since Cyrus himself was Persian. The goat, said in verse 21 to represent Greece (corresponding, then, to the leopard of the first vision), is depicted as coming with great speed from the west to destroy the ram (vv. 5-7). It had "a notable horn between its eyes," symbolizing "the first king" (v. 21). Greece did come against Medo-Persia from the west, and did so with great speed. Also it was led by the first king of the empire, the renowned Alexander the Great. Alexander's smaller forces defeated the hosts of Persia in three great battles; at Granicus in western Asia Minor (334 B.C.), at Issus in eastern Asia Minor (333 B.C.), and at Gaugamela not far from ancient Nineveh (331 B.C.).

According to verse 8, when the goat had become victorious, his "great horn was broken," symbolizing the death of Alexander. The great conqueror died in the city of Babylon at the young age of 33, after sweeping all the way to India. Following this, "four notable" horns grew in its place. This symbolizes the division of Alexander's vast holdings into four parts, under the control of four of his generals. [5] It is from one of these divisions that the little horn of this second division comes forth (v. 9).

b. The little horn as Antiochus Epiphanes. This "little horn" is correctly identified with Antiochus Epiphanes (175-164 B.C.). He was a descendant of one of these generals, Seleucus Nicator, who achieved rule over the Syrian division. There is common agreement on this identification, because this man brought extreme suffering on the Jews in Palestine. This suffering was of a nature corresponding to the descriptions, given in the following verses of this chapter, of atrocities wrought by this "little horn." Antiochus Epiphanes wanted to force the Jews to become Grecian in their thinking and practices, especially in matters of religion. He had spent time in Athens, prior to becoming king of Syria, and apparently had become enamored with the Grecian way of life. He wanted the Jews to change their Mosaic practices and

---

[5] The four divisions were: Macedonia and Greece under Cassander; Thrace and much of Asia Minor under Lysimachus; Syria and vast regions to the east under Seleucus; and Egypt under Ptolemy.

devised laws to this end. When the people resisted, they were made to suffer, with large numbers paying with their lives. The Temple was desecrated and an altar and/or statue of Zeus Olympius was erected, later referred to by Christ as the "abomination of desolation" (Matt. 24:15). [6]

In view of these matters, the reason Daniel used the same term, "little horn," for this man of ancient history as for the Antichrist of the future becomes discernable. The later little horn will be like the earlier little horn in bringing suffering on the Jews. Antiochus did this to a degree much greater than any other person of ancient time; the Antichrist will do the same to a degree much greater than any other person of future time. He was, then, a kind of antichrist of ancient time, and, therefore, appropriately called by the same term. The use of this term thus had a prophetic function. By designating this person of history as the antichrist of ancient time, Daniel was predicting the character and deeds of the Antichrist of future time. Those who would live after the period of Antiochus Epiphanes could know the general pattern of the final Antichrist by studying the life of the former one.

Thus we can learn the following information about the Antichrist. He will have the same interest as Antiochus Epiphanes in changing the religious beliefs and practices of the Jews. This is also suggested by his causing "the sacrifice and the oblation to cease" at the Temple, as noted in Daniel 9:27.[7] He will carry out this interest to the extent of employing great force, even to the slaughter of all who oppose him. And he will desecrate the Temple (which will have been restored at least by the midpoint of the tribulation) through the erection of another "abomination of desolation" (Dan. 9:27; Matt. 24:15).

3. *Daniel 11:36-39*

Our attention now turns to the second passage in Daniel which speaks directly of the Antichrist. [8] This is Daniel 11:36-39, a

---

[6] See 1 Maccabees 1:54 and 2 Maccabees 6:2. For a general description of Antiochus' atrocities against the Jews, see 1 Maccabees 1:20-61.

[7] See chapter 7, pp. 116-120, for discussion.

[8] Another possible passage, Dan. 8:23-25, is not treated here, because it speaks in reference to both Antiochus Epiphanes and the Antichrist. Dan. 9:27 will be discussed in the next chapter.

portion from the chapters recording Daniel's fourth vision (chapters 10-12). In this vision, a glorious heavenly messenger relates to Daniel events which would occur in Israel's history following Daniel's day. In Daniel 11:21-35, this heavenly messenger describes Antiochus Epiphanes, setting forth once more, in greater detail than in chapter 8, some of the anti-Jewish activities of this ruler. Then, in verses 36-45, he comes to speak of the future Antichrist. This change of subject, from the one person to the other, is evident because the description given could be true only of the future Antichrist. Verses 40-45 are mainly historical and will be discussed in the next chapter. Here we will consider the information given in verses 36-39, which concerns his character and policies.

In verse 36, the Antichrist is said to "magnify himself above every god," and to speak "marvelous things" [i.e., remarkable because they are audacious] against the true God. The verse further states that, in doing this, the Antichrist will "prosper till the indignation be accomplished," which means until the close of the tribulation period. In verse 37, he is said to turn from "the God of his fathers" (probably a reference to God as worshiped historically by Rome), from the "desire of women" (a probable reference to the finer virtues, like gentleness, mercy, and kindness, customarily associated with women), and from the worship of "any god"; and he will magnify himself above all gods. In other words, he will become atheistic in his thinking, setting himself up in the place of any supernatural being.

In verse 38, he is said to honor "the god of forces" (a better translation is "God of fortresses"[9] meaning strong military positions), a "god whom his fathers knew not." That is, he will make military strength, especially as represented by impregnable fortifications, the central interest of his life, thus making this his virtual god. He will honor this "god . . . with gold, and silver, and with precious stones, and pleasant things"; this is probably an indication that he will devote great wealth to supporting this military strength. Warfare has always been expensive, and, no doubt, will be the same in this future day.

---

[9] The word for "fortresses" (*ma'uzzîm*) is used six other times in this chapter (vv. 1, 7, 10, 19, 31, 39), either in the singular or the plural, and each time in the sense of "fortresses," not "forces."

In verse 39, the Antichrist is said to pursue his goals "in" or "against" the very strongest fortresses (the same word as in the prior verse), apparently wherever such may try to resist and hinder him. Leaders of these attacked fortresses who submit to him will be acknowledged and shown favor and will be given rule over conquered territories; this will all be under his own supreme control, of course. His purpose in this, doubtless, will be to keep a sense of good will toward him among those conquered leaders, thus channeling their talents for his benefit.

C. The "Beast" of Revelation

In the book of Revelation, the term used for the Antichrist is "beast," a designation which depicts him as ravaging and hostile to God and His will. The term is used most frequently in Revelation 13 and 17, where this person is described at some length; it also appears a total of twelve times in other chapters. [10] The discussion to follow centers mainly on the two principal chapters.

1. *Revelation 13*

Actually there are two different persons called "beast" in chapter 13. The first one, described in verses 1-8, is correctly identified with the Antichrist. The other one, presented in verses 11-18, is elsewhere called the "false prophet" (Rev. 16:13; 19: 20; 20:10). He also must be considered, because in his activities he is closely related to the Antichrist. Some Bible students, in fact, favor him for the designation "Antichrist," instead of the first beast. Some discussion will be devoted later to this matter.

a. Revelation 13:1-8. The discussion regarding the first beast in Revelation 13 significantly follows the presentation of Satan's persecution of Israel in Revelation 12. There, Satan, symbolized by "a great red dragon" (12:3), pursues Israel, symbolized by "a woman" (v. 1), for three-and-a-half years (1,260 days, v. 6; or "a time, and times, and half a time," v. 14). No indication is given as to how Satan carries out this pursuit; but now in chapter 13 the person he uses for this task is revealed in the figure of this beast, the Antichrist.

---

[10] In 11:7; 14:9, 11; 15:2; 16:2, 10, 13; 19:19, 20; 20:4, 10. Only once does the word appear in the plural (6:8), and it is not in reference to this person.

In the first three verses of the chapter, the term "beast" is used in reference to the whole empire over which the Antichrist rules. From verse 4 on, the term is used for the Antichrist personally. The usage in the first three verses is after the pattern of Daniel 7, where the entire Roman empire is symbolized by the strong, unnamed animal.

In verse 1, this beast is seen to "rise up out of the sea," like the animals witnessed by Daniel (7:3). The sea represents humanity, upon which the winds of turmoil and trouble blow. The beast has "seven heads and ten horns," a discription which identifies it clearly with the beast of Revelation 17 (vv. 3, 7). The "ten horns" correspond to the similar feature of the unnamed animal of Daniel 7, indicating that the empire in view is again Rome in its restored form, when ten contemporaneous kings will rule. In verse 2, the beast is seen to have similarities to "a leopard," "a bear," and "a lion"; these are the same three animals to which Greece, Medo-Persia, and Babylonia were likened in Daniel 7. Restored Rome will have characteristics similar to those of all three ancient empires. It is significant that "the dragon" (Satan) gives the beast "his power, and his seat, and great authority," for the Antichrist will be Satan's tool, in a unique sense, to carry out his will and program. In verse 3, the indication that one of the beast's heads was wounded to death is best understood as a reference to the demise of the Roman empire of ancient time; that the "deadly wound was healed" is a reference to the restoration of the Roman empire in the future.

With verse 4, the beast becomes personified in the Antichrist, the great ruler of this restored empire. The first indication is that the world will worship both Satan and the beast. This shows further that the two will work in unison and that many people will recognize the fact as they worship both. The growing, present-day worship of Satan, shocking and offensive as it is, prompts one to realize that the day here described may not be far in the future. In verse 5, this ruler's boastfulness is noted again, as it was in Daniel 7:8, 25, and it is described as including blasphemy against God, as observed also in Daniel 11:36. The Antichrist will rule for forty-two months—that is, three-and-a-half years, the same length of time as the last half of the tribulation period. In verse 6 his boasting is noted once more, no doubt in the interest of emphasis, but this time also with the specification that it will include the blaspheming of God's "name, and his tabernacle [the rebuilt Temple in Jerusalem], and them that dwell in heaven."

Verse 7 describes the Antichrist's oppression of God's "saints"; the expression "make war with" is used here in parallel with "wear out" of Daniel 7:25. There is no question but that the saints of God, both Gentile and Jewish, will suffer greatly at this man's hand. In the remainder of verse 7 and in verse 8, the thought is added that the Antichrist's authority will become worldwide. He will obtain power "over all kindreds, and tongues, and nations," [11] so that "all that dwell upon the earth shall worship him." The people who render this worship will be those "whose names are not written in the book of life of the Lamb slain from the foundation of the world."

b. Revelation 13:11-18. In the last half of Revelation 13, the other person designated as "beast" is described. This person, however, is called by the term only once, namely in the introductory verse of the section (v. 11). All other instances of the term, not only in 13:11-18 but throughout the book, refer to the first beast. As noted, the second beast elsewhere is called "false prophet" (Rev. 16:13; 19:20; 20:10). He is depicted in the present passage as the helper of the Antichrist, performing miracles as credentials of his authority and pointing people to the Antichrist as the one deserving their worship (vv. 12-15). He will demand that people receive "a mark in their right hand, or in their foreheads" (v. 16); this, apparently, will be a way of controlling all trade. The implication is that those who refuse this sign will not be able to buy and sell and thus will be eliminated from engaging in business and even from purchasing the necessities of life.

There is little question but that this person is a religious leader. This is indicated, first, by his designation as a false prophet. Second, he causes people to worship the first beast. Third, he is described as being "like a lamb" (v. 11). Though he is like a lamb, however, he will still speak "as a dragon," showing him to be under Satan's control like the Antichrist himself.

Since he is a religious leader and is important enough to be described in detail, he must be related to the powerful apostate

---

[11] The best texts insert "peoples" in this list, giving the overall reading: "all kindreds, peoples, and tongues, and nations." The meaning remains unchanged, however.

church. Certainly his center of activity is in Rome, and, as noted in the previous chapter, the headquarters of the apostate church is there also. Two religious powers of this magnitude could hardly be there at the same time without being interrelated in some way. The probability is that he serves as head of the apostate church. The Antichrist probably will exert his influence on the apostate group through the medium of the False Prophet, his chief assistant. As noted also in the previous chapter, the apostate church is brought to an end (Rev. 17:16) while the False Prophet continues to be active, which suggests that he effects a separation from the group in time to save himself from its fate.

It was noted earlier that some Bible students believe the name Antichrist is better ascribed to this person than to the first beast. This reasoning is based mainly on the idea that the Antichrist should be messiah-like in character. That is, if the Antichrist is to be a substitute for Christ, he must appear to the Jews as one who is acceptable as the Messiah. It is believed that the False Prophet would present this appearance in greater degree than the Roman king.

This reasoning is as follows. First, it is noted that the False Prophet rises "up out of the earth" (13:11), whereas the first beast rises "up out of the sea" (13:1). This reference to "earth" is thought to mean Palestine, thus making Palestine the residence of this person; this is believed necessary for his acceptance. Second, it is observed that this person has the appearance of a "lamb," while actually speaking "as a dragon" (13:11); this is believed to be in keeping with an intended messiah-like approach to the people. Third, Daniel 11:37 says this person will not "regard the God of his fathers." This phrase is believed to be a reference to the God of Israel's fathers. This is taken as evidence that he will be Jewish, another necessary factor for acceptance as the messiah.

These reasons are not particularly strong, however. The first, identifying "the earth" with Palestine, is weak, because there is no exegetical evidence for this identification. In fact, it seems better to take "the earth" in a general sense, since "the sea," used in regard to the first beast, carries a general meaning. The second reason, regarding the lamblike appearance of this person, does not necessarily suggest the thought of messiahship, for the Jews have historically anticipated their Messiah to be kinglike, not lamblike. The third reason, regarding the phrase "the God of his fathers," could suggest, true enough, that the person was a Jew; but as noted before, this phrase could also be a reference merely to the God whom this person's ancestors, whether Gentile or Jewish, worshiped. Moreover, as observed also in the earlier discussion, the person referred to in Daniel 11:37, where this phrase occurs, is not the False Prophet, anyway, but the first beast, the mighty king of the restored empire.

Further, as evidence in favor of the first beast being the Antichrist, rather than the second, is the fact that the idea of substitution, the principal thought in the above argumentation, is actually carried out very well in respect to the first beast. Two pertinent matters call for notice. First, this person, as king of the Roman empire, will be Satan's representative to grasp for world rule, prior to the coming of God's representative. He will be Satan's false claimant as king of the world, in substitution for God's true claimant. Second, as the king, he could have appeal to the Jews as being their Messiah. Historically, Jews have thought of their Messiah as being a king; this person, especially when he makes a meaningful covenant with them at the beginning of the tribulation, [12] could be seen by a significant number of Jews as being the Messiah. [13]

2. Revelation 17

The other chapter in Revelation presenting the Antichrist at some length is chapter 17. This chapter describes another person, a woman called the "great whore," who is seen riding on the back of the beast which represents the Antichrist. As noted earlier, [14] this woman symbolizes the apostate church, with headquarters at Rome. She is the main subject of the first and last parts of the chapter, while the beast is presented in verses 7-14.

a. Verses 7 and 8. In verse 7, the heavenly messenger, who is the speaker in this chapter, declares, "I will tell thee the mystery of the woman, and of the beast that carrieth her." The mystery of the beast is set forth first. He is described in verse 8 as the beast that "was, and is not; and shall ascend out of the bottomless pit," and again as "the beast that was, and is not, and yet is."

---

[12] See chapter 4, p. 59, and chapter 7, pp. 116-118.

[13] The subject of Messiah-anticipation is clouded by the fact that the number of Jews in Israel, looking for the Messiah, is not large. Some are, however, and these could see the Antichrist as such.

[14] See chapter 4, pp. 66, 67.

The repetition of thought here indicates a stressed importance. That importance is best related to the similar idea in chapter 13, where one of the heads of the beast was "wounded to death," after which the "deadly wound was healed" (13:3, 12, 14). This is a further reference, then, to the Roman empire of ancient history ceasing at that time and being revived in the future. The period when it "is not" is the present extent of centuries from the fall of the ancient rule until the restoration of the new one. The middle part of the verse states that when the empire reappears, it will cause "wonder" on the part of all "whose names were not written in the book of life." The word used for "wonder" (*thaumazō*) often carries the thought of "wondering with admiration." The general populace of the world will marvel at the new empire, probably because of such matters as structure, strength, and efficiency.

Twice in the chapter, the beast is described as having "seven heads and ten horns" (vv. 3, 7). This further identifies it with the beast of Revelation 13:1-8, who, in verse 1 of that passage, is described similarly. Interestingly, the "great red dragon," identified as Satan, is also described as having "seven heads and ten horns" (12:3). The significance seems to be that the Antichrist will be so empowered by and representative of Satan, in carrying out Satan's wishes, that similar descriptions are possible for both.

b. Verses 9 and 10. In verse 9, the angel states that "the seven heads are seven mountains," thus making a clear association of the beast with the city of Rome, commonly known, especially in early centuries, as the city of seven hills. [15] In verse 10, these seven heads are also said to represent "seven kings." The word for "kings" (*basileis*) may denote also dynasties or forms of rule [16] and is best so taken here. The verse further states that five of these had already fallen, the sixth then existed, and the seventh would yet arise and continue "a short space." If these "kings" were personal rulers, then the verse would make little sense, for more than five had ruled in the Roman empire by the time of John's writing; the ideas of a brief seventh and a very important eighth, as the text continues to set forth, do not fit the length and

---

[15] The hills were named Palatine, Aventine, Caelian, Esquiline, Viminal, Quirinal, and Capitoline.

[16] Significantly, the word "kings" (*malkin*) in Daniel 7:17 stands for "kingdoms," in a somewhat parallel manner.

type of rule of those following either. If the "kings" represent forms of rule, however, then the verse makes good sense. For, by the time of this writing, Rome had experienced exactly five forms of rule, [17] and the sixth then existed, namely the imperial form, which had begun with Augustus Caesar as first emperor.

c. *Verse 11.* The identification of the brief seventh "king" must be seen in the light of the strong eighth, described in verse 11. This one is said to be the "beast that was, and is not," in other words, the beast set forth in this chapter. With this eighth "king" (form of rule), then, the period of Roman rule in view must be the one of the future, when the Antichrist will be the great ruler. Because the sixth form of Roman rule, the imperialist form under the emperors, continued until Rome's fall in the fifth century, the seventh form of rule, then, must also be in this future, restored period. It is best identified with the brief period when ten kings will rule, prior to the emergence of the "little horn" of Daniel 7. The indication that the eighth form of rule is "of the seven," (better translated "seventh," [18]), is in keeping with the representation of Daniel 7 that the little horn grows up out of the midst of the ten horns.

d. *Verses 12-14.* In verse 12, the angel moves on to speak of the ten horns; and, just as in Daniel 7:24, the ten horns represent ten kings. In keeping with the other parallels with Daniel 7, these must be the same ten kings. As stated in the verse, they had indeed received "no kingdom" in the time of this writing, but would receive power at the time of the beast's dominion for what is called "one hour." In view of all that has been seen, this "one hour" must be the seven years of the tribulation, when the Antichrist enjoys his time of rule. Verse 13 adds that the ten kings would "give their power and strength unto the beast," a statement fully in keeping with the other passages studied. Verse 14 states that these, along with the beast, will "make war with the Lamb." This Lamb can only be Christ, and the occasion must be when Christ comes in power at the close of the tribulation, bringing full defeat on the Antichrist and these helpers.

---

[17] They were the rulerships of kings, consuls, dictators, decemvirs, and military tribunes; see Barnes, *Notes on the New Testament, Revelation,* pp. 422-424 for extensive discussion and references.

[18] The word used can also mean "seventh" (cf. Matt. 22:26) and is best so taken here.

D. The "Man of Sin" of Second Thessalonians 2

The third term used for the Antichrist is "man of sin," found in Second Thessalonians 2. Though this chapter has already been investigated in part in a prior discussion, it is necessary now to consider it for what it teaches regarding the Antichrist.

1. *Verses 3 and 4*

The term "man of sin" actually appears only once, in verse 3. Paul there says that the person so called must make his appearance at the very beginning of the tribulation, for he will provide one sign that this period has begun. Paul's point to the Thessalonians was that, because this person had not yet appeared, they could know that the tribulation had not yet begun. Paul continues to speak in some detail regarding the man of sin. In verse 4, he states that he will oppose and exalt "himself above all that is called God, or that is worshipped"; this is quite similar to what is said in Daniel 11:37. Paul adds however, that "he as God sitteth in the temple of God, shewing himself that he is God." This will probably occur when the Antichrist has invaded Israel and conquered Jerusalem and the Temple there. Apparently, he will be audacious enough to take a seat in the sacred building, as if he were the god for whom it had been built.

2. *Verses 6-9*

In verse 6, the thought is set forth that a certain power has continued down through history to prevent the Antichrist from appearing sooner. This power is designated as "what withholdeth," which is best taken as a reference to the Holy Spirit. [19] So, then, because the Holy Spirit has continued His work of restraining sin in the world, Satan has been unable to work his wiles through the Antichrist. This implies that Satan's plan will call for the existence of unrestrained sin, when human beings can be brought to exercise the vilest thoughts and actions. In verse 8, it is plainly stated that, as soon as the Holy Spirit ceases in this work of restraint, the wicked one will be revealed. In the same verse, Paul adds the thought, noted previously, that this one will be consumed by Christ, "with the spirit of his mouth" and "with the brightness of his coming." In verse 9, the work of the Antichrist is tied

---

[19] See chapter 5, pp. 88, 89 for discussion.

in once more with that of Satan, who is said to give him power to perform "signs and lying wonders." This is a reference, no doubt, to the miracles performed through the instrumentality of the False Prophet, as described in Revelation 13:13-15. These power displays will serve as deceiving credentials, which will convince even those who should know better, having previously been taught and warned in the present age, to become followers of this wicked person (v. 10).

E. Summary Statements

It is appropriate at this point to list in brief summary statements the principal information concerning the Antichrist as described in the passages treated.

1. The Antichrist will be the final king of a restored form of the Roman empire.

2. He will come to power at a time when a confederacy of ten rulers has already been formed, displacing three of these at the time. The remaining seven will then assist and support him as head ruler.

3. He will come to power at the beginning of the tribulation period, providing a sign that it has begun. This will coincide with the time when the Holy Spirit ceases His work of restraining sin in the world.

4. He will be a capable person with keen insight, but extremely boastful, even daring to blaspheme the name of God and to try to change basic laws of nature.

5. He will be empowered and controlled by Satan as no other person of history has been.

6. He will be assisted by one called the False Prophet, who is also empowered and controlled by Satan.

7. The False Prophet will be subordinate to the Antichrist and will cause people to worship this head of state, deceiving them by miracles wrought through power granted by Satan and forcing them to receive an identifying mark in order to buy and sell.

8. The Antichrist will work through this False Prophet, the head of the Rome-centered apostate church, to bring severe persecution on true saints, even bringing about martyrdom for many.

9. Toward the close of the tribulation period, he will destroy the apostate church, for which he will then no longer have use. However, he will spare the False Prophet, who has been its head; apparently this one will show himself quite willing to disassociate himself from the apostate church of the time.

10. The Antichrist will remain in power during all seven years of the tribulation, continuing to ascend in power for approximately the first half of the period and exercising the height of this power for the last half, during which time he will enjoy worldwide authority in some real sense.

11. Religiously, he will show his atheism by denying the existence of all gods and will assume the position of a god himself. He will call for people to worship him and will take a seat in the Temple of God in Jerusalem, after conquering the Holy Land.

12. As the driving interest of his reign, he will make military strength his virtual god, especially during the years of his ascendancy in power. He will undertake offensive campaigns against opposing rulers and then will solicit the support of those rulers by distributing favors.

13. His three biblical names are significant: "little horn" depicting him as a king, growing up among and displacing other kings; "beast" presenting him as possessing a ravaging, animallike nature; and "man of sin" portraying him as given to, permitting, and advocating sin in the world, instead of exalting the finer virtues of life.

14. His name, Antichrist, is significant, not only because he will be antagonistic to Christ and His righteous standards, but because he will be a substitute for Christ. He will be Satan's false claimant to world rule prior to the appearance of God's true Claimant, Jesus Christ.

15. The Antichrist, the False Prophet, and the Roman empire will all be brought to an abrupt end by Christ when He comes in power as the Messiah-Deliverer of the nation of Israel, at the conclusion of the tribulation period.

Questions for Review

1. In what passages of Scripture is the term "antichrist" used?
2. What two meanings does the term "antichrist" have?
3. Show the symbolic significance of the four animals used in Daniel 7 to represent the four empires.
4. What part of Daniel 7:7 gives evidence that there will be a restored form of the Roman empire? Explain.
5. Summarize what is taught regarding the Antichrist in Daniel 7: 7, 24-26.
6. What is the symbolic significance of the two horns on the ram in Daniel 8?
7. What is the symbolic significance of the one horn and then the four horns on the goat in Daniel 8?
8. Of whom is the little horn of Daniel 8 symbolic? Describe him.
9. What is the significance of this person being called "little horn" like the Antichrist of Daniel 7?
10. Who is described in Daniel 11:21-35? In 11:36-45? How may one know that the person represented changes?
11. Summarize the main features set forth regarding the Antichrist in Daniel 11:36-45.
12. What is the symbolic significance of the term "beast" being used for the Antichrist?
13. Who is the beast of Revelation 13:1-3? Summarize the main descriptive points.
14. Summarize what is taught regarding the beast in Revelation 13:4-8.
15. Who is the beast of Revelation 13:11-18? Summarize what is said about this person.
16. Review the arguments for and against identifying the beast of Revelation 13:11-18 with the Antichrist.
17. What evidence is found in Revelation 17:8 for the idea of the Roman empire being restored?
18. What twofold significance is there for the seven heads of the beast, as set forth in Revelation 17:9-11?
19. Summarize matters taught concerning the Antichrist in Second Thessalonians 2:3-9.

7

Israel
in the
Tribulation

Our attention now turns to the experience of Israel during the tribulation. In previous discussions, the tribulation has been considered primarily as endured by the world at large, with only an occasional reference to Israel. Now, the role of suffering encountered by the Jews is to be discussed. Again, several key scripture passages should be studied.

Before beginning the study of these passages, a word of explanation is in order as to the possible time of fulfillment of the prophecies to be explored. As has been noted, there is no way to know at what time the rapture of the church will occur and the tribulation will begin. As will appear in the following discussion, however, the information presented in these key texts fits the world situation existent today remarkably well, suggesting that the time may be soon. This is true particularly in respect to the contemporary Israel-Arab conflict and the resulting Russian-Arab alignment. For this reason, the discussion will occasionally refer to these present realities as if the predicted events will occur while they still exist. It should be understood, however, that God's timetable may call for the matters predicted to be fulfilled at a time still further removed. If this should be the case, the world situation then will fit the picture just as well, though it may perhaps be characterized somewhat differently. It is precarious and unwise to become too specific. Still, because the

present situation does fit so well into what these texts call for, I
have chosen to write as I do, though with the reservation indicated.

A. Daniel 9:27

The first passage to be noted is Daniel 9:27, which is the con-
cluding verse in the passage relating Daniel's third vision. This
vision was discussed in chapter four for the purpose of showing
that the tribulation period will last seven years. Israel's relation
to the period was mentioned only incidentally. Now this relationship is the main interest, as the last verse of the passage is studied.

As noted in the earlier discussion, verse 27 specifies two important time-indications in respect to Israel's relation to the Antichrist. The first is that the Antichrist will establish a covenant or
treaty with Israel at the beginning of the tribulation week. The
other is that he will break it at the midpoint of the week, as
signified by his causing "the sacrifice and the oblation to cease"
at the Jerusalem Temple. The first will inaugurate a period of
safety and security for Israel, lasting until the middle of the week;
the latter will begin a period of severe suffering, continuing for
the remainder of the seven years. Each division of the total period
calls for consideration.

1. *A treaty with Israel*

The first period begins with a covenant or treaty. This agreement need not be thought of as some covenant of history, now
revived. Some expositors have thought this to be so, because the
King James Version employs the definite article, as though this
were a covenant known previously. The Hebrew does not use
the article, however, but speaks only of "a covenant" (*berîth*).
The probability is that this will be a new covenant, desired and
agreed upon by both the Antichrist and Israel, of a mutual-respect,
non-aggression type.

a. The rationale for such a treaty. The desire for a treaty
of this kind is understandable, from the point of view of both
Israel and the Antichrist. Israel as a nation is looking for friendly
nations today and probably will be in the future. Israel does not
have many friends. At one time, Russia was a friend; this is
evidenced by Russia's vote for the partition of Palestine, to which
the Arab nations were strongly opposed, in the fall of 1947.
France was a staunch friend for many years, even selling Israel
many fighter planes after 1948. This changed, however, after the

Six Day War of 1967, when France suddenly refused shipment of planes ordered that year. The United States remains Israel's friend today, but only with caution. In this light, it is easy to see that Israel would be glad for a show of friendship by such an important figure as this king of the restored Roman confederation.

One can see how the Antichrist would want such a treaty also, in the light of the present world situation. Today, Russia and the Arab block of nations are aligned against Israel. Should this alignment continue until the Antichrist arises, he could well see it as a threat to his expansionist designs. This might easily lead him to desire friendship with the central opponent of this threat, thus seeking to restrain the ambitions of the opposing group. He might also have another purpose in mind: the securing of Palestine for himself in due time. Palestine's strategic position could be attractive to him, as well as the vast mineral wealth of the Dead Sea; he might look upon such a treaty as a holding device until he would be ready to make his own attempt for the land.

b. The duration of the treaty. Verse 27 indicates that the Antichrist makes this treaty with Israel to last one week, that is, seven years, as made clear in the earlier discussion. [1] This week also is the seventieth in the total seventy predicted through Daniel, during which God would effect certain things in Israel's history (9:24). There is no reason to believe that the Antichrist will be aware of this significance, when he proposes that the treaty last for this length of time. It is probable that he will merely see seven years as an appropriate period for which to establish it. In this, however, he will provide one more example of how God can employ even wicked men to carry out His program.

c. The benefit for Israel. As long as the Antichrist continues this treaty, Israel will have reason to rejoice. To have a partner of this strength, against the Russian-Arab bloc, will be a pleasant change from the past. There will suddenly be little reason to fear an invasion of the land. Border disputes will assume a different character, as Israel will now find full support for her cause. The people will be able to relax considerably from the historic interchange and struggle with the Arab nations. Annual expenditures for military programs will become greatly reduced, with monies now made available for educational and social benefits. The people of the land will have reason to believe that their fortunes have

---

[1] See chapter 4, p. 58.

greatly improved, and this will cause them to be highly favorable toward the Antichrist and his program.

2. *The treaty broken*

This happy situation will completely change, however, at the midpoint of the seven-year period. The text states that "in the midst of the week" the Antichrist "shall cause the sacrifice and the oblation to cease." In view of the remainder of the verse, this must mean that he will break his covenant with Israel at this time by ordering the ceremonial program to cease. His reason for wanting to make this change will appear in the next passage to be considered. This verse only notes his change in attitude and the nature of the oppression he will inflict on the Jews.

a. Sacrifice and offering made to cease. A first matter to consider is the way in which the Antichrist will indicate this breaking of the treaty; that is, by ordering the cessation of the sacrificial ceremonies. The implication is that he will have been opposed to the ceremonies before this, but will make his attitude known only at this time. This opposition is understandable. The Antichrist will be an atheist, and he will find all worship of a personal deity objectionable. This feeling may even be intensified in respect to the Jews, since they will probably show a greater dedication in their worship than any other people in the sin-characterized world of that day.

The reference to sacrifices indicates that the Jews will have restored Temple worship by this time. No clear indication is given in Scripture regarding the date of this restoration. Perhaps the most likely time would be during the three-and-a-half years preceding this order. These years, as has been noted, will have been characterized by peace and security, when attention could be given to a major project of this kind. More money, also, would be available, with military expenditures having been reduced.

b. The desire to rebuild the Temple. The question may well be raised as to the desire of the modern state of Israel to rebuild the Temple and reinstate a ceremonial system. Is it realistic to think that such a desire will exist? I believe that it is. The Temple and its services were basic to Israelite life all the time of ancient history, as long as the people were in their land. Sacrifices were conducted regularly, up to the time of the Temple's destruction by the Romans in A.D. 70. Since that time, furthermore, a continuing feature of orthodox Jewish worship has been to call on God to renew the "days as they once were." This would include a plea for restoration of that which had been central during those days. It is logical to believe that when the opportunity comes, the people of Israel will rebuild the Temple.

Even though the nation had been reconstituted since 1948, the Temple could not be rebuilt prior to 1967, because the Temple area was not yet in Jewish possession. It has not been possible to rebuild it since that time, either, because of the continuing obstruction of the Dome of the Rock, which has been on the Temple site since the seventh century. Today, however, Israel wants to effect the reconstruction should the opportunity arise. A lead religious article appeared in a national, secular periodical only three weeks after the Six Day War, carrying the significant title, "Should the Temple Be Rebuilt?" Jewish leaders quoted were quite sure that it both should and would be rebuilt, indicating that the question concerned only the time and manner. The main obstacle noted was the existence of the mosque. When asked, how this might be removed, one Israeli historian replied, "Who knows? Perhaps there will be an earthquake." [2]

c. The suffering inflicted. The verse (Dan. 9:27) continues by telling of developments which come as a result of breaking the treaty. Two points are noted. The first is indicated by the words, "for the overspreading of abominations he shall make it desolate"; this can also be translated, "even unto the overspreading of abominations of desolation." The phrase rendered "abominations of desolation" is in essence the same as used by Jesus in Matthew 24:15 (cf. Mark 13:14); He certainly was referring to this verse. [3] It is also the same phrase as used of an object erected in the Jerusalem Temple by Antiochus Epiphanes (Dan. 11:31). Antiochus erected a substitute altar and/or statue to Zeus (Jupiter) Olympius, and ordered Jews of the time to worship this Grecian deity. The significance of the name as used by Daniel is that the object was an "abomination" in the sight of God, and it served to make the Temple desolate because no more worshipers would come. The "antichrist" of ancient history, Antiochus Epiphanes, erected such an object in his day; and this verse says that the

---

[2] "Should the Temple Be Rebuilt," *Time,* June 30, 1967, p. 56.

[3] Daniel uses the phrase again in reference to the tribulation period, in 12:11; but that instance presupposes this one, making this the likely one to which Jesus referred.

Antichrist of the future day will do the same, also making the Temple desolate then.

The second development is indicated by the words, "even until the consummation, and that determined shall be poured upon the desolate"; again this can be better translated, "and unto the end even what has been determined shall be poured out upon the desolate." The word for "consummation" or "end" logically refers to the close of the tribulation time. The thought of the phrase is that, during the last half of the tribulation week, all the desolating activity which God has determined beforehand will be fully poured out upon Jerusalem, making it desolate. The nature of this activity is not explained, but a general idea can be gained by a comparison to what Antiochus Epiphanes did in his day [4] and from other passages which will be discussed later in this chapter. The total picture is one of terrible suffering, inflicted on the Jews by the Antichrist after he has broken his covenant with them.

B. Daniel 11:40-45

As indicated in the previous chapter, all ten verses of Daniel 11: 36-45 concern the Antichrist. At that time the first four verses were discussed, because they present the character and policies of this future ruler. Now the last six verses hold our interest, for they describe his historical activity.

1. *A major war*

The first historical action noted, which is a major one, concerns a war. Verse 40 says a "king of the south" will push at the Antichrist, and a "king of the north shall come against him like a whirlwind, with chariots, and with horsemen, and with many ships." This war will take place "at the time of the end." In view of the context, this is a clear reference to the tribulation period. The first antagonist against the Antichrist is called "king of the south." Both this term and that given to the other enemy, "king of the north," have been used in the early verses of Daniel 11 in reference to the Ptolemaic and Seleucid kings of ancient history, ruling Egypt and Syria, respectively. It is noteworthy that Egypt is still strong today and, in fact, the leader of the Arab bloc of

---

[4] See chapter 6, pp. 101, 102.

nations. In terms of current history, then, "king of the south" could well refer to Egypt's ruler, as the leader of the Arab world.

2. The "king of the north"

More must be said regarding the identity of the "king of the north," for the present Syrian government hardly fits as a world contender, in the stature of the ancient Seleucid rulers. The common view is that a replacement is intended here, and two positions are held by expositors as to his identity.

a. Two positions as to identity. One position is that this king is the Antichrist himself, for which two arguments are presented. First, he is the most likely candidate, since he is the central subject of the context. Second, he is the most logical candidate, since he was typified by Antiochus Epiphanes, one of the former kings of the north. The other position is that this king is the leader of the present nation of Russia. This second view must be preferred, in the light of several convincing arguments.

b. Evidence against the Antichrist being this king. First, the designation used for the Antichrist when he is introduced in this passage (v. 36) is not "king of the north," but rather the shorter term "the king." One would expect the more characteristic designation there, if it were attributable to him. Second, though Antiochus Epiphanes did typify the Antichrist, he did so as an individual and not as a member of the Seleucid line. Also, he is himself, significantly, not called by the term "king of the north." Third, the designation "king of the north" does not fit as well for the Antichrist, as for a Russian ruler, because geographically Russia is straight north of Israel with Moscow being almost on a direct north-south line with Jerusalem, while Rome is mainly west.

c. Evidence in favor of the Russian leader. Positive evidence in favor of a Russian ruler being this king may be taken from a parallel passage, Ezekiel 38, 39. First, in these two chapters a great battle is described which must transpire during the tribulation period, as shown by several factors: (1) it will occur after the Jews have returned to their land (38:8, 12); (2) it will be in "the latter years" (38:8) and in "the latter days" (38:16), both phrases referring to the tribulation time; (3) it will be when the returned Jews are living in a sense of peace and safety (38:11), which could well be sometime during the three-and-a-half year period of the treaty with the Antichrist (Dan. 9:27); and (4) it must occur before Christ has destroyed all Israel's enemies

(Zech. 14:1-3; Rev. 19:11-21), for such an attack as here described could hardly take place after that.

Second, the above factors seem to indicate that the battle must be closely related to, if not identical with, the battle of Daniel 11:40, because they both occur during the tribulation period; two totally different battles could hardly transpire in so short a time in the same general area. [5] Third, a close relation or identity between the two battles is evidenced also by the probability that the Antichrist would want to become involved if Russia should attack Israel, since the Antichrist will have a peace treaty with the smaller country. He would want to protect the interest for which he had made the treaty. Fourth, the king involved in the battle of Ezekiel 38 and 39 can be properly identified with the ruler of Russia for two reasons: (a) his domain is said to be Magog, Rosh, Meshech, and Tubal (38:2, 3), names of Old Testament people living in northern Mesopotamia and the Caucasus region, who, as is commonly accepted, migrated north into Russia to make up much of its present populace; [6] and (b) his country is described as being in the "uttermost parts of the north" (38:6, 15; 39:2, literal Hebrew), which identifies him with the far north, where Russia is. A fifth argument is that this northern king allies himself with Persia, Ethiopia, and Libya (*paras, kush, put,* Ezek. 38:5; cf. 30:5; Nah. 3:9) in this battle; these countries could represent the same Arab bloc of nations as are led by the "king of the south."

d. Two other arguments in favor of the Russian leader. To these arguments, two others of a different type may be added. One is that, on the basis of grammar, it can be expected that the "him" of the phrases "at him" and "against him" of Daniel 11:40 should refer to the same person. This is true, if they are taken in reference to the Antichrist. But then the Antichrist cannot be identified with the "king of the north." The other is that an identification of this "king of the north" with a Russian ruler makes good sense in terms of contemporary history. When the Antichrist makes a covenant with Israel, at the beginning of the tribulation

---

[5] Especially when at least the one battle must take place approximately at the midpoint of the tribulation, as will be seen.

[6] For evidence and source reference, see J. Dwight Pentecost, *Things to Come,* pp. 326-331; John F. Walvoord, *The Nations in Prophecy,* pp. 105-108.

week (Dan. 9:27), the Arab bloc of nations could be expected to seek Russia's help, lest all hope of obtaining the land be lost. Russia could be expected to respond favorably, too, in an attempt to offset the rising challenge of the Antichrist. The Antichrist, with his ambitious plans, would of course retaliate against such a rival alliance, especially if war should be declared against himself or Israel.

e. The weapons used. The weapons indicated as being used in the struggle, "chariot," "horsemen," and "many ships," could well be representative of modern instruments of war, Gunpowder, planes, rockets, missiles, and atomic bombs were quite unknown in biblical time, and people would have been confused if specific reference to them had been made. No doubt, in some part, "ships" and "horsemen" will actually be used, but the thought need not be that only these will be employed.

3. *Victory for the Antichrist*

The victor in this battle is indicated in the closing words of the verse: "And he shall enter into the countries, and shall overflow and pass over." The antecedent of "he" is clearly the Antichrist, who is the subject of the entire section. The "countries" must include Palestine, the "glorious land" of the following verse, and also Egypt, Libya, and Ethiopia, designated in Daniel 11:42, 43. The words "overflow and pass over" carry the image of a river overflowing land. The words show that the conquest is decisive and complete; the Antichrist is now able to move into and through these other countries. He wins complete victory over the Russian-Arab bloc. In view of matters noted in the parallel passage, Ezekiel 38 and 39 (especially 39:2-20), it is clear that this victory is accomplished as a result of God siding temporarily with the Antichrist. One might wonder at this, but the probable reason is that this victory is necessary since God has a purpose yet to be served by this wicked person, in connection with His people Israel. He is to be the instrument for bringing them to a proper attitude of humility for accepting Christ as their Messiah-Deliverer.

4. *Invasion of Palestine by the Antichrist*

In verse 41, the victorious Roman ruler is said to "enter into the glorious land," a definite reference to his entry into Palestine. [7]

---

[7] The same phrase is used for Palestine in Daniel 11:16 and 8:9.

Having been victorious in the preceding battle, the Antichrist will find the way clear to lay claim to Palestine for himself. This he will do by way of invasion, apparently soon after the prior victory. This indication gives a helpful clue as to when, during the tribulation week, the struggle with the Russian-Arab bloc will occur. Because the Antichrist does not break his covenant with Israel until the midpoint of the period (and such an invasion as this could hardly occur until it had been broken), the time of the struggle could not be later than shortly before that midpoint. There would be good reason, too, for the Russian-Arab alliance to desire to fight against the Antichrist relatively soon after he makes his treaty with Israel, certainly at least within the three-and-a-half years of the first half of the tribulation. Also, such a victory achieved by the Antichrist, with the resulting desire to invade Palestine, could well provide the impetus for him to break the treaty. Thus the most probable time for this stuggle is just before the midpoint of the tribulation, with the breaking of the covenant and the invasion of Israel coming directly after.

Verse 41 says further that "many . . . shall be overthrown." The King James Version inserts "countries," but the Hebrew text does not have this word, and the context does not call for it. The Antichrist does not overthrow "countries" when he invades Palestine, but people. The meaning is that, on pushing into the land, many Jewish people are overthrown. It is at this point, then, that the oppression of the Jews, at the hand of the Antichrist, will begin. Until this time, the Jews, as a nation, will be favorable toward the Antichrist, probably even helping him in the preceding battle. [8] But now they will have their opinion suddenly and rudely changed, being forced to see him for what he truly is: an aggressor interested only in his own benefit. No doubt, they will staunchly try to stem his advance, but their army and air force, worthy as they are today, will prove no match for his powerful war machine. They will have to retreat continually, as many die in the onrush. Finally they will see their land fall completely under the Antichrist's control.

The latter part of verse 41 states that countries to the southeast of Palestine, those which occupy the land of ancient Edom,

---

[8] This is implied in the story as told in Ezekiel 38 and 39, in that the Jews are presented as those against whom the alliance comes.

Moab, and Ammon, will not be invaded, following the fall of
Palestine. The next two verses indicate why.

5. *Invasion of Northeast Africa*

According to these verses (42, 43), the reason for the Antichrist not invading southeastward is that he moves southwestward.
He advances down into northeast Africa, where he conquers
Egypt, Libya, and Ethiopia. It is not difficult to see his reasoning in this. He will have just defeated the Egyptian army, in
the recent struggle over Palestine, leaving the country of Egypt
defenseless. The text states that "the land of Egypt shall not
escape"; the Antichrist will seize control of the gold, silver, and
precious things there. Having taken Egypt, he will move westward to seize Libya and southward to take Ethiopia.

According to verse 44, the Antichrist, while yet in Africa,
will hear disturbing news from "the east" and "the north," and
he will immediately "go forth with great fury to destroy, and
utterly to make away many." Bible students differ on the nature
of this news. Some believe that it will concern information relative
to an invasion of 200,000,000 warriors from the far east (Rev.
9:16), under the leadership of "kings of the east" (Rev. 16:12).
The thinking is that this vast horde of soldiers will have heard
of the Antichrist's victory over the earlier north-south confederacy
and will now want to challenge him for world leadership. [9] Perhaps a more probable view, however, is that the news will concern
primarily reverses which his own troops, left as garrisons in
Palestine, will have experienced at the hand of Jews, who will
suddenly have risen up and started fighting again.

Arguments against the first view and in favor of the second
are as follows. First, the former view finds much of its ground
in a particular interpretation of Revelation 9:16 and 16:12, [10]
which may not be correct. Second, the figure of 200,000,000

---

[9] This view is held, for example, by Pentecost, *Things to Come*, pp. 356-
357 and Walvoord, *Daniel the Key to Prophetic Revelation*, pp. 279-280.

[10] This interpretation holds that the verses depict an army of 200,000,000
men crossing the Euphrates, dried up for the purpose, to invade the Palestine area. As noted in chapter 4, p. 63, however, the 200,000,000 of Revelation 9:16 may well be demons, in that their weapons are fire, smoke, and
brimstone. Also, the "kings of the east" of Revelation 16:12, for whom
the Euphrates is dried up, are actually depicted as helping the Antichrist
(Rev. 16:13, 14), rather than fighting against him.

for an army of human soldiers is almost beyond comprehension, especially in terms of the logistics involved in traveling all the way from the far east. Third, the latter view seems more plausible because an uprising by supposedly defeated Jews in Palestine is what one might expect, for the Israelis of today have demonstrated a spirit of enthusiasm in combat almost unexceeded in history. Fourth, the Antichrist, on returning to the land, is able "to destroy, and utterly to make away many"; this can be understood of a comparatively small Jewish force, but hardly of an army of 200,000,000.

6. *Palestine crushed*

In verse 45, the conclusion of the Antichrist's efforts in Palestine is set forth, succinctly but forcefully. The words just quoted from verse 44, that he is able "to destroy, and utterly to make away many," show that, upon returning to the land, he fully annihilates the last of Jewish resistance. Having accomplished this, he is able to "plant the tabernacles of his palace between the seas in the glorious holy mountain." He will be able, as a mighty conqueror, to erect his private residence in the country, both as a symbol of imposed domination and as a base from which to effect his new controlling authority. The "glorious holy mountain" is Mt. Zion, or Jerusalem, and the "seas" are the Mediterranean Sea and the Dead Sea. The broad thrust of the words is that the Antichrist's victory over the Jews of Israel will be full and complete. The efficient army and air force, of which the people are so proud today, will have been totally destroyed. The land, and especially the city of Jerusalem, will lie in ruin.

The closing words of the verse state that, in due time, the Antichrist will also be brought to his end. This, as the next chapter shows, will be effected by Christ, when He comes in glorious power to deliver His people, now fully humbled and ready to receive Him as their Messiah.

7. *The battle of Armageddon*

The name "battle of Armageddon" is commonly and properly given to this great struggle between the armies of the Antichrist and the Jews. The name is taken from Revelation 16:16, which falls in the descriptive passage concerning the outpouring of the sixth vial of wrath. Verse 14 speaks of the "whole world" being gathered "to the battle of that great day of God Almighty," to a "place called in the Hebrew tongue Armageddon." "Armageddon" is best taken to mean "hill of Megiddo." Megiddo was a strong city of Israel, some seventy miles north of Jerusalem, known widely as a place of great historic battles. [11] The name suggests that at least some aspect of this future battle will be fought there.

A question arises at this point, however. Certainly the battle against the Jews climaxes at Jerusalem, not Megiddo. How can both places be involved in the same struggle? The answer is best found in considering the name being used in reference to a continuing war and not one battle. In fact the word used in Revelation 16:14, translated "battle," is *polemos* which is commonly distinguished from the parallel word *machē* as signifying a war rather than a battle. [12] Since war between the forces of the Antichrist and the Jews will have been quite continuous from the midpoint of the tribulation, it may be that the name should be applied to the entire struggle of these three-and-a-half years. To account for the name, one may believe that the early part of the continuing war will have been fought at or near Megiddo, with its later stages taking place at Jerusalem.

The possibility exists that the battle between the Antichrist and the Russian-Arab bloc will be the opening aspect of this overall war. [13] This early struggle will be fought within the confines of Palestine, for those who die will do so on "the mountains of Israel" (Ezek. 39:4; cf. vv. 9-15). And the city of Megiddo, within the land, is as likely a place for this battle as any. Perhaps, then, that part of the overall war which gives the name Armageddon to it is this opening battle between the Antichrist and the Russian-Arab bloc, fought at Megiddo. In the light of Revelation 16:12, which speaks of the Euphrates River being dried up for the coming of "kings of the east," it must be that kings of the Mesopotamian area become involved in the war at some point. Possibly, on seeing the Antichrist victorious in the struggle against the alliance they will choose to cast their fortunes with

---

[11] For instance, it was here that Josiah, king of Judah, was killed trying to hinder Pharaoh-nechoh of Egypt from going north to Carchemish to do battle with the Babylonians (2 Kings 23:29, 30).

[12] See Richard C. Trench, *Synonymns of the New Testament,* pp. 322-324.

[13] Another possibility is that, following this early struggle, the first contacts made by the Antichrist with Israel's forces will be at Megiddo.

him. This would swell the ranks of the Antichrist to a still greater number and make even more meaningful the indications that those ranks would come from "all nations" (see Zech. 14:2).

C. Conversion of the Jews

A further significant feature of the tribulation period is that substantial numbers of Jews will be converted. (The conversion of a large number of Gentiles was observed in chapter four.) The intent now is to look at passages which speak of this fact. It should be recognized that numerous texts speak only generally regarding the matter. That is, they refer to the total number of Jews who will turn to Christ, whether during the tribulation period or at its close, when Christ will come to deliver them from the Antichrist. For instance, this is the import of Romans 11:26, "And so all Israel shall be saved." The salvation of "all Israel" will occur only after Christ's grand coming in power, as the next words of the same verse indicate: "There shall come out of Sion the Deliverer, and shall turn away ungodliness from Jacob." This general meaning is found also in Isaiah 4:3, 4; Jeremiah 23:5, 6; 24:7; Ezekiel 36:25-27; 37:23; Zephaniah 3:11, 12; Zechariah 13:1, 2. We are not concerned now with these passages, however. Their significance will be pertinent in the next chapter, when the climax of the tribulation period is the subject. Our interest here concerns texts which speak particularly of Jews who are saved during the tribulation period.

1. The 144,000 of Revelation 7:1-8 and 14:1-5

The first two texts speak of 144,000 Jews, who clearly are saved during this seven-year span of time.

a. Revelation 7:1-8. One of these is Revelation 7:1-8, in which this sizable group of Jews is first presented. In the movement of events set forth in Revelation, the time of this presentation comes after the opening of the sixth seal. As seen in chapter four, [14] this means at the midpoint of the seven years. In the first verse of the passage, four angels are seen "standing on the four corners of the earth, holding the four winds of the earth," so that they will not bring their devastating effects on the earth.

---

[14] See chapter 4, pp. 61, 62.

Another angel is directing the first four to continue holding back these winds until "the servants of our God" have been sealed in their foreheads. These servants are identified as the 144,000 of interest here. Following verses indicate that this total number is made up of 12,000 from each of Israel's twelve tribes, [15] thus identifying the total group unmistakably as Jews.

The text gives two reasons for this sealing. The first is that the 144,000 are thus identified for protection against the "four winds" of destruction. The primary nature of this destruction follows logically from what happens in the succeeding chapters, namely, the damage coming from the blown trumpets and poured-out vials of wrath. [16] In fact, in Revelation 9:4, the specific instruction is given that the fifth blown trumpet is to hurt "only those men which have not the seal of God in their foreheads." These 144,000, then, will be spared in large part from the suffering so represented. [17] The second reason is that the 144,000 are thus signified as true believers in God. They are called "the servants [bondslaves] of our God," indicating that they serve God, which calls for true faith in Him. Also, the act of sealing, used for identifying, carries in itself the implication of ownership and security. In addition, the second passage noted, Revelation 14: 1-5, presents the group clearly as constituted of redeemed people.

b. Revelation 14:1-5. That the same group is referred to in this passage follows from its identification again as 144,000. A number of this kind would hardly be used for two different groups in the same book. The time at which the group is viewed here, however, is later than in the former passage — probably near, or even after, the close of the seven-year period. It is important to note the evidence presented in the passage that the members

---

[15] Since the twelve tribes listed include Levi, one must be omitted, and this is Dan. Some expositors believe that the reason for Dan's omission is to be found in Dan's having moved from its allotted territory (Judges 18).

[16] For discussion, see chapter 4, pp. 62-65.

[17] It has been noted in earlier contexts (chapter 2, p. 30; chapter 4, p. 60) that all the nation of Israel will probably be spared in large part from these punishments, designed especially for the Gentile world (see Isa. 26: 20, 21). The reason why the 144,000 should be selected particularly for protection here is not clear. Perhaps they enjoy a greater degree of protection, and possibly they will be given special care in view of the Antichrist's oppressions as well.

of the group are redeemed people. There is first the fact that they are said to have the "Father's name written in their foreheads" (v. 1);[18] this factor seems to indicate also the type of seal in reference in the previous passage. Second, they alone are able to learn a song which is sung "before the throne" of God (vv. 2, 3). Third, they are described as "redeemed from the earth" (v. 3). Fourth, they are those "which follow the Lamb whithersoever he goeth" and are "redeemed from among men, being the firstfruits unto God and to the Lamb" (v. 4). Fifth, they are without fault before the throne of God," because "in their mouth was found no guile" (v. 5).

c. Redeemed Jews. These 144,000, then, will be redeemed Jews, from each of the twelve tribes. The sealing seems to take place at the midpoint of the seven-year time. This suggests that their conversion will occur during the first half of the period, because this sealing does not indicate the time of conversion, but only the identification of those already converted. It seems clear, then, that at least 144,000 Jews will be converted during the first three-and-a-half years of the tribulation. It should be noted that the actual number may be still larger. Some expositors believe that the number 144,000 is only symbolical, signifying a larger group, with the intention of showing that every tribe of Israel will be represented in sizeable number. Other expositors take the number literally, but still believe that the total company of believers will be larger, seeing the 144,000 as designating only those especially active in witnessing for Christ. [19] I personally am inclined toward the first of these views.

2. *The two witnesses of Revelation 11:3-13*

Another passage calling for attention in this matter is Revelation 11:3-13, which presents "two witnesses" as prophesying through a period of 1,260 days during the tribulation.

a. Identity. Many expositors believe that one of these two witnesses can be identified with Elijah, here returned to earth at this future time. Evidence is drawn from the following factors. First, Malachi predicted this great prophet would be sent "before the coming of the great and dreadful day of the LORD" (Mal.

---

[18] The best manuscripts read, "having his name, and the name of his Father, written on their foreheads."

[19] For discussion, see Pentecost, *Things To Come,* pp. 297-301.

4:5), [20] Second, fire is said to proceed out of the mouths of these
two witnesses, similar to the time when Elijah called down fire from
heaven to destroy men sent by Israel's King Ahaziah (2 Kings 1:
9-14). Third, the two have power to restrain the heavens from sending rain, similar to the power exercised by Elijah when rain was
withheld for a period of three years and six months (James 5:17).

The other witness is often identified with Moses. Evidence
is found in the power of the two witnesses to turn water to blood
and "to smite the earth with all plagues" — things which Moses
did while on earth. Other expositors identify the second person
with Enoch. Evidence here is taken from the fact that he was the
only other person, besides Elijah, who did not die. It is thought
appropriate if these two, who do experience death in this future
time (Rev. 11:7), had not died previously, thus avoiding the idea
of their having to die twice. If the two persons are to be identified with people of past history, probably two of these three
are the most probable candidates.

Because the two are not named, however, the possibility
exists that they are not to be identified with any historic person,
but will simply live for the first time at this future date. If this
should be the correct view, the two clearly would be outstanding in
faith and courage, daring to witness for Christ in the face of the
gravest difficulty. Their power to work miracles, then, would
probably be due to their remarkable degree of dedication.

b. Time of activity. The duration of the activity of these
two witnesses will be 1,260 days (11:3), which is forty-two months
or three-and-a-half years. Because this duration corresponds exactly to one-half of the tribulation, and because the last half of the
tribulation is specifically in the immediate context (11:2), [21]
it is logical to conclude that this witnessing activity takes place
during that period. These two people, whatever their identity,
will begin their work at the time when the Antichrist breaks his
treaty with Israel and will continue throughout the difficult months
of his oppression and persecution. The unusual power with which

---

[20] This could be taken to mean, however, only that one would come
in the spirit of Elijah, which seems to be the thought conveyed in respect
to John the Baptist fulfilling this promise (see Matt. 11:14; Luke 1:17).

[21] In v. 2, Jerusalem is said to be trodden under foot 42 months, which
must be a reference to the Antichrist's oppression. This comes in the last
half of the tribulation week.

they are endowed by God will be necessary so that they will be able to continue, since the Antichrist surely will oppose them with the greatest severity.

c. *Empowered by the Holy Spirit.* According to 11:4, the two witnesses are "the two olive trees, and the two candlesticks standing before the God of the earth." This is a reference to Zechariah's vision of the olive trees and the candlestick in Zechariah 4. The message there concerns Zerubbabel and Joshua and their need for empowerment by the Holy Spirit. A parallel thought is no doubt intended here. That is, these two witnesses of the future will need and will experience a similar empowerment from the Holy Spirit for their faithful and courageous task of witnessing, as well as for the working of miracles. The number and type of miracles gives some indication of the degree of their power. They will be able to devour enemies by fire from their mouths, to shut up the heaven from giving rain, to turn water to blood, and to impose numerous plagues (11:5, 6).

d. *Death and resurrection.* According to 11:7, the death of the two witnesses occurs only after they "have finished their testimony." In view of the indicated duration of three-and-a-half years, this must be at the very close of the total seven-year period. The verse continues to say that, at that time the beast (Antichrist), who will by this time have established his palace in Jerusalem (Dan. 11:45), will be permitted to "overcome them, and kill them."

Verses 8-10 tell the reaction of the people when this has happened. Verse 8 states that the dead bodies of the two will not be buried but will be left to lie openly on the streets of Jerusalem, evidently as a way of showing disdain for the two. Verse 9 indicates that people of various nationalities will see their dead bodies for a period of three-and-a-half days, possibly through the medium of television, which could indeed be seen the world around by satellite transmission. Verse 10 adds the shameful note that people, on seeing them, will rejoice and make merry, because the two prophets had "tormented them." Since the people seem to include Jews of Israel, as well as Gentiles from the world at large, it follows that the two witnesses will have to override opposition, not only of the Antichrist, but the people to whom they will be trying to minister. This is surprising, for one would think that their fellow Jews would not treat them thus, since the Antichrist will be the enemy of both. All this adds to the idea that these two will indeed be courageous men in the spirit of the great prophets of old.

According to verses 11-13, honor will be bestowed on the two at the end of the three-and-a-half-day period of lying dead on the streets. In verse 11, they are resurrected to life and stand suddenly to their feet, causing fear once again among the people observing them. In verse 12, they are taken directly to heaven, while their enemies still watch. In verse 13, a great earthquake occurs, which brings destruction to a tenth of the city and death to no less than 7000 people. This makes the overall occasion even more memorable and results in people at last giving "glory to the God of heaven."

e. Significance. The point of this account, in respect to the conversion of Jews, is that a witness for God will exist during the entire last half of the tribulation. Because at least 144,000 will be converted during the first half, this means that all seven years of the week will see faithful witnessing being carried on. That only two witnesses are identified for the last half of the period does not mean that they will be the only ones active. They should be thought of, rather, as the outstanding witnesses of the time, with their very leadership inspiring others to engage in the same task.

The total picture is that the number of Jews who will turn in faith to Christ during the seven-year period will be quite large. Probably the first Jews to turn will do so as a result of reading Bibles and religious books — something true also in respect to the Gentiles, as noted in chapter four. These in turn will witness to others, and finally the 144,000, or more, will be converted. Most of these, no doubt, will continue to live on into the last half of the period. Others will certainly join their number as a result of the witnessing of the famous two as well as of the 144,000. Martyrdom will come for many, especially during the oppressions of the last half of the period. These, along with martyred Gentiles, will constitute those described in Revelation 20:4 as "the souls of them that were beheaded for the witness of Jesus and for the word of God." [22]

---

[22] Martyrs are depicted also in Revelation 6:9, shown as a result of the fifth seal being opened. The time then is just before the midpoint of the tribulation. If these martyrs include Jews, as well as Gentiles, then some martyrdom will have occurred for them already in the first half of the period.

D. Persecution of the Jews

The fact that Jewish persecution is involved in the tribulation period has been indicated in various ways in the preceding discussion. There are certain passages, however, which speak specifically of this, and these call for consideration at this point.

1. *Jeremiah 30:7*

Notice first Jeremiah 30:7, which gives the well-known name to the period, "the time of Jacob's trouble." The verse reads: "Alas! for that day is great, so that none is like it: it is even the time of Jacob's trouble; but he shall be saved out of it." The context speaks of suffering experienced by Israel. The time of this suffering refers in part to the Babylonian captivity of Judah, but, as is true of many passages, it refers also to the suffering of the tribulation time. This is made evident by indications such as in verse 9, that after this suffering is over, the people will "serve the LORD their God, and David their king," whom God will raise up unto them. Verse 10 says that then the people will return and "be in rest, and be quiet, and none shall make [them] afraid." These developments did not occur after the return from Babylon, but will occur in the future. Another indication that this suffering refers to the tribulation is the phrase, "so that none is like it" (v. 7). Only one time can be worse than any other, therefore this phrase must refer to the same period as that referred to by the expressions which occur three other times in Scripture: Daniel 12:1; Joel 2:2; Matthew 24:21 (cf. Mark 13:19).[23] Designated here as "the time of Jacob's trouble," this period is shown to be characterized especially by trouble for Israel. The nature of the trouble is not identified in the verse, but its fact is made clear. Other passages show that it will consist of hardship, difficulty, unpleasant conditions, deprivations, loss of life, and anything which comes under the general term, "trouble."

The closing phrase of the verse, "but he shall be saved out of it," is explained further in verse 11: "Yet will I not make a full end of thee: but I will correct thee in measure, and will not leave thee altogether unpunished." The "trouble," then, does not result in annihilation of the people, for the nation will continue. The point is made that an important purpose will be served by

---

[23] See chapter 4, p. 54.

this suffering. The people will be corrected. They will learn a lesson. As noted in prior discussions, this discipline is needed that the people might be made willing to receive Christ as their Messiah-Deliverer. The Jews of Israel in the present day are not ready to receive Him. For the most part, they have returned to the land in unbelief, and today they are interested in what they as people can do and make for themselves. A radical change is needed if they are to open their minds and hearts to Him in the future day. A basic purpose of the tribulation "trouble" is to bring this about.

2. Revelation 12:1-6, 13-17

a. Explanation of the passage. A second passage to note is Revelation 12:1-6, 13-17. In the opening verses, a woman, symbolic of Israel, and a great red dragon, symbolic of Satan, are presented. The woman is at the point of giving birth to a child, symbolizing Christ, and the dragon stands ready to devour him as soon as he is born. The historical occasion symbolized is Jesus' birth into the world. At that time Herod the Great, as Satan's tool, issued his directive that all male children, two years and younger, should be killed in an attempt to take the life of Jesus (Matt. 2:16). In verse 5, the child is said to be "caught up unto God"; this represents Christ's ascension following His life on earth. Between verses 5 and 6, an extended gap of time must be recognized, because in verse 6 the woman is described as fleeing "into the wilderness," where she is protected and nourished for 1,260 days; this is a reference to the last half of the tribulation week.

In verses 8-12, the main story concerning the persecution of the woman is interrupted by an account of the dragon, Satan, being cast from heaven. Then with verse 13, the story continues, noting further the fact of this persecution. In verse 14, the woman is again said to flee "into the wilderness," where she is cared for during a period described as "a time and times, and half a time." This formula has been explained in another connection [24] to mean three-and-a-half years, or 1,260 days, the same length of time as given in verse 6. The occasions are identical, then. Verses 15 and 16 speak of Satan trying to kill the woman, who

---

[24] See chapter 6, p. 100.

has fled, by a flood of water, but the earth helps the woman by swallowing the flood. This flood should be understood symbolically, as representing whatever means of destruction Satan, working through the Antichrist, will bring against Israel during this last half of the tribulation. Verse 17 concludes by stating again, generally, that the dragon was angry with the woman, adding that this anger was directed especially against those who kept "the commandments of God," meaning true believers.

b. Meaning of "wilderness." A question arises whether the term "wilderness" is to be taken literally or symbolically. That is, does the passage mean that the people of Israel will flee literally before the invasion of the Antichrist, that they will leave Palestine and go into the desert to the east (or, as some believe, south to the old Nabatean fortress of Petra)? Or, does it mean that the people will find themselves forced symbolically into a wilderness of suffering, where they will be protected, not by flight, but by God's gracious care? Those who hold to the first possibility argue not only from the language here, but from Jesus' words in Matthew 24. In Matthew 24:16, speaking about this same period of time, Jesus says, "Then let them which be in Judea flee into the mountains"; in verse 20, He says the people should pray that their "flight be not in the winter, neither on the sabbath day."

Those who hold to the second position, however, find even more convincing evidence. They note, for instance, that if the Jewish people flee in large number, there would not be enough of them left in the land for the Antichrist to destroy two-thirds of their number, as Zechariah 13:8, 9 indicates. In addition, the two witnesses of Revelation 11 would have few people to whom to preach; their preaching must be done in Jerusalem since their dead bodies lie on Jerusalem's streets for three-and-a-half days (Rev. 11:8, 9). Zechariah 14:2, which speaks of this general time, not only tells of Jerusalem as a physical city being destroyed by the Antichrist during this time, but of women within the city being "ravished" and half the populace being taken captive. This again means that fighting is done within the land, not outside in some desert area. It is difficult to think of Jews, at least as represented in the land today, fleeing from anyone, even the Antichrist. They are courageous, confident, and zealous to hold every square foot of the soil which has finally become theirs. Further, passages which speak of Christ delivering the Jews from the Antichrist, at the climax of this time, imply that Jews will be on hand to acclaim Him at that time. No intimation is given in any pertinent passage that they will have to return from a far-off place to receive Him. Rather, the picture is of people who have been duly impressed by having witnessed the deliverance at first hand, and thus are brought to the appropriate frame of mind for receiving Christ.

c. Significance. The significance of this passage is that it clearly describes Israel's persecution during the last half of the tribulation period. Included are several items of information regarding this persecution, which may be summarized as follows. First, Satan will be the one who masterminds the persecution, working through the instrumentality of the Antichrist. Second, the persecution will continue for 1,260 days, that is, the last half of the tribulation period. Third, Satan's bitterness against Israel will be increased as a result of his being cast from heaven, [25] apparently just prior to this period of persecution. Fourth, during this time Israel will be protected from annihilation, shown symbolically by God preparing a place for her in the wilderness (v. 6), by her being cared for there (vv. 6 and 14), and by the earth opening its mouth to swallow the flood of the dragon (v. 16). Fifth, the dragon, in his anger at the woman, makes war especially on true believers among the Jews.

3. *Zechariah 13:8 and 9; 14:1 and 2*

A third passage is Zechariah 13:8, 9 and 14:1, 2. The book of Zechariah, from chapter 12 on, speaks principally of last-day events. In 13:8, 9, it gives the number of Jews who will be destroyed by the Antichrist as two-thirds of the populace, leaving only one-third. Today there are almost three million Jews in Israel. If there are the same number by the time of this persecution, no less than two million will be destroyed.

In Zechariah 14:1 and 2, the attack by the Antichrist on the capital city of Jerusalem is depicted. The statement is made that the city will fall, the women will be ravished, and half of the

---

[25] This occasion of Satan being cast from heaven contrasts with the time set forth in Isaiah 14:12-17; at the earlier time, he was cast from heaven as his regular place of abode, while still being permitted to return for the purpose of accusing the saints (Job 1:6-12; 2:1-7; Rev. 12:10), while here he is cast out fully, not being permitted to return for any reason.

city will be taken captive. [26] Obviously, such words speak of terrible suffering. If Jerusalem will be treated this way, other cities may be expected to endure the same. All told, the degree of carnage and slaughter implied in these verses is quite beyond one's ability to imagine.

In 13:9, the significant result of this persecution is stated, a result which emphasizes God's purpose in permitting the shocking event. The verse states that the surviving one-third of the people, who will be brought through the "fire" of the suffering, will experience a refinement and a testing, such as that applied to silver and gold in the smelting process. This will lead them to call on God's name, and God will respond by accepting them as His people. In other words, the pride found among the people of Israel today will be removed, along with their lack of willingness to receive Christ as their Messiah. They will be made willing to do whatever God wishes and will accept their great Deliverer.

4. *General summary*

A summary of the total suffering experienced by the people of Israel during the tribulation is in order. We will not only relate information from the three passages, but also discuss the significance of the parallel provided by the ancient ruler Antiochus Epiphanes.

a. Major suffering, at the hand of the Antichrist, will begin for all Israel following the Antichrist's defeat of the Russian-Arab alliance and the resultant broken treaty with Israel, which will occur at the midpoint of the tribulation period.

b. This suffering will come first in the form of direct warfare, as the Antichrist invades the land, apparently meeting and defeating Israel's army and air force and then moving on to seize Jerusalem.

c. In the pattern of Antiochus Epiphanes, his counterpart of ancient history, he will probably at this point force compliance to his earlier order relative to the cessation of Temple ceremonies. It probably will be at this point also that he will erect his "abomination of desolation" in the Temple, which could be an image of himself before which he will demand Jewish worship. Along with

---

[26] No contradiction should be seen between this figure of "half" and the "two-thirds" of 13:8, for this figure refers only to the city of Jerusalem, while the other has in view the entire land.

these offensive orders, which the Jews will vigorously protest, will be measures of punishment which will result in the slaughter of thousands.

d. During this time, the courageous two witnesses will be carrying on their ministry, encouraged by believers but hated by all others, including the Jews themselves. Through their activity, however, numerous Jews will turn in faith to Christ, to join the ranks of the 144,000, most of whom will probably still live.

e. After the initial victory of the Antichrist, he will move with his major force southwest into Africa, to subjugate Egypt, Libya and Ethiopia, leaving only controlling garrisons in Palestine. At this time, the Jews will make one last effort to throw off his recently imposed bondage by attacking these garrisons. This will infuriate him, prompting him to return quickly and put down the insurrection more severely than at the first occasion of fighting. Once more Jerusalem will be taken, so that the Antichrist can and will place his tent of victory there. From there he will continue to impose intense suffering until two-thirds of the people are killed and Jerusalem, the capital, is left in complete ruin.

Questions for Review

1. What is the probable nature of the covenant mentioned in Daniel 9:27?
2. What rationale may be given for this covenant being made?
3. For how long a period of time is the covenant made?
4. What benefit will Israel enjoy while this covenant is in force?
5. By what action will the Antichrist break this covenant?
6. Do the Jews today wish to rebuild the Temple? Explain.
7. According to Daniel 9:27, what will the Antichrist do in Palestine during the last half of the tribulation week?
8. Who are the participants in the war set forth in Daniel 11:40?
9. Summarize the evidence which shows that the "king of the north" of Daniel 11:40 is the leader of Russia.
10. Who is victor in the battle of Daniel 11:40? Give evidence.
11. At what point in the tribulation week does this battle probably take place? Give reasons for your answer.
12. Review what Daniel 11:41 teaches regarding the Antichrist's actions directly after this victory.
13. What countries does the Antichrist invade after Palestine?
14. Why does he hurry back to Palestine again? Discuss.
15. Describe Israel's final fall to the Antichrist.
16. Why should the great battle be called the "battle of Armageddon"? Discuss.
17. At what point in the tribulation week are the 144,000 sealed?
18. For what two reasons are the 144,000 sealed?
19. Who are the 144,000? Tell what you can about the group.
20. What possibilities exist as to the identity of the two witnesses of Revelation 11:3-13?
21. During what part of the tribulation week are the two witnesses active?
22. Describe what happens at their death and resurrection.
23. Will there be other witnesses for Christ to the Jews besides these two? Explain.
24. Summarize what Jeremiah 30:7 says regarding Jewish persecution.
25. Summarize what Revelation 12:1-6, 13-17 says regarding Jewish persecution.
26. Discuss the meaning of the term "wilderness" in this passage.
27. Summarize the teaching of Zechariah 13:8, 9 and 14:1, 2 about the suffering of the Jews.

8

The Close
of the
Tribulation

The tribulation period is brought to a close by the coming of Christ in power to deliver the surviving Jews from the Antichrist. This coming is often called the revelation of Christ. It terminates not only the seven-year period, but also the rule of the Antichrist and the very existence of the restored Roman confederacy. It thus sets the stage for Christ to establish His own true rule of the world. With Satan's false ruler deposed, God's proper Ruler can take the throne. The point of this chapter is to consider scripture portions which tell of this coming of Christ and of the factors involved in making the transition from one rule to the other.

A. Christ Comes in Power

The first passages to notice are those which speak directly of Christ coming in power. Three are especially significant.

1. *Zechariah 14:3 and 4*

The first is Zechariah 14:3, 4, which is a continuation of a passage treated earlier, concerning the extent of suffering imposed by the Antichrist. Verse 3, continuing from a statement concerning the capture of Jerusalem by the Antichrist, declares, "Then shall the LORD go forth, and fight against those nations, as when he fought in the day of battle." This sets the time of Christ's coming as shortly after the complete subjugation of the city. Christ will wait until all seems hopeless for the Jews, and then come upon the scene. By this time, the Jews will realize that their own strength is insufficient. Their own defensive forces will be devastated. Their leadership, capable as it is today, will have proven inadequate. Their native ingenuity, of which they are presently so confident, will have been found lacking. Nothing will be left in which to find encouragement. By this time, too, the Antichrist will think himself completely adequate for any challenge. Having defeated all his enemies, he will think that his work lies behind him, with only the spoils of the recent war calling for any attention.

On the actual day of Christ's arrival, the Antichrist will be gathered with his army, perhaps in a victory celebration, in the "valley of Jehoshaphat" (Joel 3:2, 12); a valley best identified with the Kidron, [1] located between Jerusalem and the Mount of Olives. Then it will be, says the verse, that "the LORD shall go forth, and fight against" the nations gathered under the Antichrist's banner.

In verse 4, the specific place where Christ will return at this time is identified. It will be the Mount of Olives, from which He left nearly two thousand years ago. On that former occasion He was speaking to the disciples, when "a cloud received him out of their sight" (Acts 1:9). It is only fitting that He should return to the same place. The verse continues by speaking of a tremendous physical phenomenon, which will occur at His arrival: the cleaving of the mountain from east to west, as "half of the mountain shall remove toward the north, and half of it toward the south." Such an event, apparently coming just as Christ's feet touch the earth, will cause all witnesses to be enormously impressed. The power and authority of the One who has just arrived will be made strikingly clear, both to the enemy in the valley and to the Jews observing from Jerusalem.

---

[1] Some identify it with the "valley of Berachah" (2 Chron. 20:26), for there Jehoshaphat enjoyed the spoils of a great victory; but this is rather far to the east. Others suggest an identification with the miraculously opened valley through the Mount of Olives (Zech. 14:4), but this is not formed until Christ actually comes, and would hardly be large enough to suit the need, anyway.

2. *Matthew 24:27-30*

The second passage to consider is Matthew 24:27-30, which falls within the Olivet Discourse. In this discourse, Christ relates the sequence of last-day events. There are two other records of the discourse; in these, the portions which parallel these verses in Matthew are Mark 13:24-26 and Luke 21:25-27. Just prior to this section of the discourse, Jesus speaks of the reality of the tribulation period (Matt. 24:21) and of the claims of false christs who will then exist (24:23-26). From these thoughts He moves on in the present section to describe His true appearance, indicating that it would be of a nature that could not be mistaken.

In verse 27, Christ states that His coming will be very noticeable, like the "lightning" coming "out of the east" and shining "even unto the west." When lightning spreads across the sky in this manner, it is indeed noticeable. He emphasizes the point by an illustration in verse 28, speaking of the hunting eagles gathering wherever prey is to be found. When birds of prey circle overhead, they are noticeable to observers on the ground. In verse 29, two points are made. The first is chronological: Christ's coming will be "immediately after the tribulation of those days." This is in accordance with other passages already studied. The other is phenomenological: remarkable events will occur in respect to nature. The sun shall be darkened, "the moon shall not give her light, and the stars shall fall from heaven, and the powers of the heavens shall be shaken." [2] Events of a similar nature will have occurred already at the midpoint of the tribulation, as has been seen (Rev. 6:12, 13). The effect of such events will be to draw men's attention and let them know assuredly that something of unusual importance is about to happen. God clearly will make the moment of Christ's arrival on earth very noticeable. Such events will also bring an attitude of awe and fear, which will provide a proper setting for Christ's arrival.

In verse 30, Christ introduces His actual coming with the words, "Then shall appear the sign of the Son of man in heaven." When these tremendous displays of nature have occurred, Christ will come. The word "sign" is best taken as roughly equivalent to the word "sight." The Antichrist, with his hosts, having seen

---

[2] Some expositors take these developments figuratively, standing for political changes, but the context calls for a literal interpretation.

the signs of nature, will suddenly look up and see the amazing "sight" of Christ approaching, accompanied by His hosts. [3] The sight will prompt the "tribes of the earth" to mourn. Probably, this mourning will come mainly from the national groups assembled in the Antichrist's army, who will have reason to mourn and become concerned lest their victory be not so complete after all. The view of the Conqueror coming "in the clouds of heaven with power and great glory" will be reason enough for their anxiety.

3. *Revelation 19:11-21*

The third passage to note is the most informative of the three, Revelation 19:11-21. The passage falls in the book of Revelation after the descriptions of the tribulation scenes involving the broken seals, the blown trumpets, and the poured-out vials of wrath. In the immediately preceding verses (19:5-10), the marriage supper of the Lamb has been described. [4] The time, then, is at the close of the seven-year period.

a. The coming in glory. In verses 11-16, the scene of Christ's actual descent to earth is depicted. Verse 11 describes heaven being opened; from it a "white horse" comes forth, with One sitting on it called "Faithful and True." He is said to come in "righteousness" to "judge and make war." The rider on the horse is Christ, the only one who can be called "Faithful and True" in the ultimate sense. Verse 12 describes His eyes as "a flame of fire," signifying keenness of insight and knowledge. He is adorned with "many crowns," showing the deserved honors that have been granted Him (cf. Rev. 4:10). The verse states further that "he had a name written, that no man knew." No clue is given for knowing what name is in reference, and no reason exists for conjecture. Verse 13 indicates that his "vesture" appeared as if it had been "dipped in blood"; a reference either to Christ's work of blood-atonement, at His first coming, or to the shedding of blood in judgment of Antichrist's army, soon to be effected. [5] The verse then gives another unmistakable name for Him, "The Word of God."

---

[3] Christ's hosts are identified later in the discussion (under Rev. 19:14) as consisting of angels and glorified saints.

[4] See chapter 3, pp. 51, 52 for discussion.

[5] See also the idea of Christ's treading the winepress in v. 15 (cf. Isa. 63:2, 3; Rev. 14:20), which depicts the pouring out of God's wrath.

Verse 14 turns to the subject of those who accompany Christ. These also ride on "white horses" and are "clothed in fine linen, white and clean." Whiteness generally symbolizes purity in Scripture. This host, then, is pure from sin. Other passages indicate that the makeup of the host is twofold: first, the church, now glorified, judged, and married to the Lamb; and, second, angels (Matt. 25:31) who come to render service as needed. When one thinks of the total number of Christians from all centuries who will be in this group, besides the many angels probably involved, the size of the host takes on immense proportions. Certainly the appearance of this grand coming will be a sight to impress all observers on earth.

Verse 15 pictures Christ prepared for the coming judgment. "Out of his mouth" proceeds a "sharp sword, that with it he should smite" the army of the Antichrist, effecting complete dominance over him and his subjects "with a rod of iron." The figure of Christ treading out "the winepress of the fierceness and wrath of Almighty God" shows strikingly the nature of this judgment. As men tread grapes in a winepress, bringing stains of the crushed grapes high on their garments, so will Christ tread out the blood of guilty men. The last matter noted in the description is the identification of a name written both on Christ's "vesture," already said to have been "dipped in blood," and on His "thigh": the name is "KING OF KINGS, AND LORD OF LORDS," the highest possible. Christ alone is worthy of it, and He is ascribed with it as He comes here in power on this momentous occasion.

b. The defeat of the Antichrist. The last five verses of the passage describe the defeat of the enemy host. Now that Christ has come, this defeat is His first business. The description shows two divisions.

The first part (vv. 17, 18) is parenthetical in thought. It interrupts the story to state, by means of gruesome symbolism, that soon there will be a great number of dead bodies of men lying on the earth. The verses depict an angel crying with a loud voice for "all the fowls that fly in the midst of heaven" to come to "the supper of the great God." This supper consists of human flesh. It is called the supper of God because it is God who provides it; that is, He brings about the deaths of the men whose bodies provide the food for the birds to eat. The bodies are set forth according to their rank in the army. There is the flesh first of "kings," those who had served under the Antichrist and had been his supporters from the beginning; then the flesh of "captains," the leading military figures under the kings; third, the flesh of "mighty men," vital in their service to the captains; fourth, the flesh of "horses, and of them that sit on them," the horsemen; and, lastly, the "flesh of all men," meaning all others, including footmen and assistants. The use of the word "all" is to say that none escape. All suffer extinction at the hand of Christ.

Verse 19 resumes the story, giving the second division of the section. It tells of the victory over the forces of the Antichrist, particularly setting the scene of the opposition Christ faces. This opposition consists of the "beast" (Antichrist), the "kings of the earth" under him, and their armies — a vast host of people. They are "gathered together to make war against" Christ and His army. The thought seems to be that the Antichrist and his forces, having been relaxing outside Jerusalem, look up now to see the approach of Christ's great throng; accordingly they quickly rise up and prepare to fight. The resulting conflict, however, if it can even be called that, is short-lived. The next verse moves on to tell of its results, and it does not mention any fighting at all.

The fate of both the beast and false prophet is first noted. These two leaders are cast directly, while still alive, into "a lake of fire burning with brimstone," meaning hell (cf. Dan. 7:11). The two, then, are not permitted even to pass the normal portals of death, apparently in the urgency for their consignment to eternal hell. Interestingly, they thus become the third and fourth persons in history who do not die; the first two were Enoch (Gen. 5:24; Heb. 11:5) and Elijah (2 Kings 2:11). But, in contrast to these great men of faith who were highly honored, the Antichrist and the False Prophet will be severely dishonored, for this action will only serve to bring them the more quickly to the punishment they deserve. This, then, is the reason why they are not listed in verse 18 among those providing food for the birds. They do not die as the others. This also is the "end" of the Antichrist to which Daniel referred (11:45) when he said so correctly that there would be none to help him in that day. Note that the False Prophet is carefully identified, being described as the one who did miracles before the Antichrist. This lets the reader know that this man is truly the same as the one in Revelation 13:11-17, where he is similarly described.

Verse 21 tells of the fate of the armies of the Antichrist. They suffer a more normal end, being "slain," apparently as they stand together in the valley. The instrument Christ uses is said to be the "sword," noted both in verse 15 and now again as proceeding "out of his mouth." This probably is figurative language for Christ's voice of authority. That is, Christ's words will go forth like a sword of destruction to cause their deaths. This is the reason for the brevity of the conflict. The Antichrist's hosts rise to fight, but with swords only drawn and not used, they fall in death. Those in Christ's great army act only as observers, apparently not needing to fight at all. The last part of the verse returns to speak of the fowls. They are filled with the flesh for which they have been called to come and eat.

4. *Summary*

The principal points made in the above passages may be summarized as follows:

a. The time of Christ's coming will be just as the Antichrist has brought Israel to its point of lowest humiliation, with two-thirds of the people killed and Jerusalem fully in ruins. The Antichrist will be with his vast army in the valley of Jehoshaphat (probably the Kidron, at the foot of the Mount of Olives), thinking that his victory is complete and relaxing in the glow of accomplishment.

b. Suddenly, he and his host, along with the defeated Jews who survive in the city of Jerusalem, will witness miraculous changes in nature in respect to the sun, moon, and stars, which will alert all observers that something of major importance is about to occur.

c. Then these people will view the grand spectacle of Christ coming in glory, along with His enormous throng, approaching the earth from above, all in the dazzling whiteness of purity.

d. They will witness the arrival of this host on the Mount of Olives, at which time they will be amazed by a sudden movement of the mountain, as a gaping valley is formed, running through it from east to west.

e. About this time, the Antichrist will issue orders for his troops to prepare for battle against this heavenly army. It would seem that these troops, being only mortal and sinful, in such contrast to the pure-white host from heaven, would not want to fight; but apparently they still will obey and rise as commanded.

f. Having risen, however, they will not have any opportunity to fight. Even as they make their preparations, they will witness the miraculous removal of their two main leaders, the Antichrist and the False Prophet, and they themselves will fall in death.

g. The Antichrist and the False Prophet, having been snatched from their army, will find themselves cast into the torment of eternal hell, without having been taken through the normal portal of death.

h. The many bodies of the slain troops will lie exposed on the open field, available as food for birds.

i. Christ and His twofold army will not be involved in actual fighting, but will remain victorious on the Mount of Olives, overlooking the scene of death stretched in the valley below. They will also be in sight of the capital city, Jerusalem, then in ruins but soon to become the leading city of the world.

B. Preparation for the Kingdom

With the defeat and removal of the Antichrist and his supporting people, the way will be cleared for the establishment of Christ's millennial kingdom. In Rome, any attempt by lesser leaders to choose a replacement for the departed Antichrist will be short-lived at best. This will be true both because the army and probably most of the potential leaders will have been killed at the Mount of Olives, and because Christ's supreme presence on earth will soon become known far and wide. Between the moment of the Antichrist's defeat and the actual inauguration of the millennial reign, however, several matters will necessarily transpire. Passages which tell of these intervening events will now be considered.

1. Jews in Israel accept Christ as Messiah

Much of what has been stated in previous points of the discussion implies that the Jews in Israel will accept Christ as their Messiah when He comes in power to deliver them. Because this thought is basic in the overall presentation, it is necessary to verify it from a few appropriate passages.

One such passage is Zechariah 12:10, which, speaking generally of the end-time, says, "And I will pour upon the house of David . . . the spirit of grace and of supplications: and they shall look upon me whom they have pierced, and they shall mourn for him, as one mourneth for his only son." This mourning will evidently be in lament for what the Jews did to Christ at His first coming. Further in the same book (13:9), God says through Zechariah that the result of the tribulation suffering will be that the people "shall call on my name, and I will hear them: I will say, It is my people: and they shall say, The LORD is my God."

Another passage to notice is Ezekiel 36:24-31, where God states that, after His people have been gathered from all countries and brought to their own land, He will "sprinkle clean water" upon them, so that they will be clean from all filthiness and idols; He will also grant them "a new heart" and put His spirit within them. The result will be that the people will remember their "own evil ways" and "loathe" themselves for their iniquities and abominations.

Still another passage is Isaiah 25:9, "And it shall be said in that day, Lo, this is our God; we have waited for him, and he will save us: this is the LORD; we have waited for him, we will be glad and rejoice in his salvation."

A final passage is Romans 11:26, where Paul declares, "And so all Israel shall be saved." The time of this salvation will be when "there shall come out of Sion the Deliverer, and shall turn away ungodliness from Jacob."

These and similar passages make clear that the surviving Jews in Israel will give their allegiance, apparently unanimously, to Christ as their Messiah. As has been seen, many will already have done this prior to Christ's coming in power. The others will do so when they witness the wondrous deliverance Christ effects for them from the control of the Antichrist.

2. *A judgment of Jews*

A few passages speak of Jews being judged at this time, with many being counted as rebels. How can these passages be fitted with the ones just noticed which depict the Jews of Israel, as a group, accepting Christ? The answer is best found in connection with Jews who will have continued to live in other parts of the world, outside Israel. Today many Jews live in countries other than Israel, especially in the United States. Many of them will apparently want to transfer their residence to Israel at this end-time. The judgment depicted in these passages seems to concern them, at least primarily. Two passages are especially significant.

a. Ezekiel 20:33-38. The first is Ezekiel 20:33-38. It is appropriate, initially, to note evidence that the passage does speak of the posttribulational time. First, the passage concerns a general time when God will rule over the Jews (v. 33). Second, this time will be when Jews are brought back from countries where they have been scattered (v. 34). Third, it will be a time when all Jews "in the land" will serve God and be accepted of Him (v. 40). Fourth, it will be a time when they will loathe themselves because of their previous sinfulness (v. 43). The only time in history when all this will be true will be following the close of the tribulation period.

In the middle of this passage the prophet speaks of a judgment. He states that the Jews in question will be judged (Hebrew, *shaphat* [6]) by God in "the wilderness" (v. 35), as God judged the "fathers in the wilderness of the land of Egypt" (v. 36). He adds that God will cause these people to pass under His rod and will bring them "into the bond of the covenant" (v. 37). Some will thus be purged out as rebels, namely those who transgressed against the LORD; they will not be permitted to enter "the land of Israel" (v. 38). The prophet's intention is to draw a parallel between Israel's experience in the wilderness, when the people travelled from Egypt to Canaan, and this future time of the return of Jews from the various outside countries. As Israelites were judged earlier, due to their unbelief especially at Kadesh-barnea (Num. 13, 14), and made to wander and die in the wilderness as punishment, never entering the Promised Land, so these Jews of the future, who wish to return to Israel, will be judged, with at least some being turned back as rebels and kept from entering the land.

The parallel suggests the reason for this. The people judged as rebels will be those who have not given their allegiance to Christ. The Jews already in the land will all have accepted Christ by this time. This presents a further rationale for this judgment. God will want only those who have placed true faith in Christ to be citizens of the land. Therefore, those who have not done this will not be welcome. This does not mean that all who wish to enter the land at the time will be turned away. The land will have room for many additions, especially since two-thirds of the

---

[6] The Hebrew *shaphat* is the usual word for the idea "to judge" all through the Old Testament.

people will have been killed by the Antichrist. No doubt, many of those who apply for entrance will qualify and will be made welcome.

b. Malachi 3:1-5. The other passage is Malachi 3:1-5. It is not as explicit as the former passage, but does substantiate the idea of this occasion of judgment. The particular time in view is again established by the context as being the close of the tribulation period. The portion presents Christ, "the messenger of the covenant" (v. 1), as one who brings judgment like a "refiner's fire" (v. 2). This characterization fits Christ well at this posttribulational time of judgment. Those judged are said to be "the sons of Levi"; the purpose of the judgment is to prompt these "sons" to "offer unto the LORD an offering in righteousness" (v. 3). A special reference certainly is intended to priests and Levites of the day, those literally descended from Levi; they will be required to perform sacrifice and offering at the rebuilt Temple in the proper manner. In a broader sense, however, it would seem that Jews in general are also in view, to the end that they might present an "offering in righteousness" to the LORD, in the sense of exhibiting righteous conduct in their personal lives. In His millennial kingdom, Christ will require righteous lives on the part of all citizens. It seems logical that the Jews referred to here, whether taken in the general sense or particularly as priests and Levites, are posttribulational returnees to the land, as in the previous passage. As noted above, those already in the land will have professed true faith in Christ and will not need this time of judgment.

3. *A judgment of Gentiles*

The days immediately after the deliverance of Christ will witness also a time of judgment for Gentiles. The purpose will be, as with the Jews, to make selection of those who will be privileged to enter the glorious millennial period. Two passages especially call for consideration.

a. Matthew 25:31-46. The first passage is Matthew 25: 31-46. In verse 31, Christ is described as coming "in his glory." The following judgment, then, must take place at the close of the tribulation. At that time, He shall "sit upon the throne of his glory," judging "all nations" gathered before Him, separating "sheep" from "goats" like a shepherd. The word for "nations" is *ethnos,* which can be translated "Gentiles" as well as "nations," and should be so translated here. God's judgment is on an individual basis, not national. Those individuals judged to be "sheep" are permitted to "inherit the kingdom," meaning, in the light of the context, the millennial kingdom (v. 34); those judged to be "goats" are sentenced to "everlasting fire, prepared for the devil and his angels" (v. 41). This last reference indicates that the issue concerns not only the identity of kingdom inhabitants, but also the later and eternal inhabitants of heaven (v. 46).

Most of the passage is concerned with the nature of the test used in making the judgment. In brief, the test involves the attitude of each person toward the "brethren" of Christ (v. 40), meaning the Jewish people. If the person has been willing to feed, clothe, and give shelter to the Jews, he is accounted a "sheep," but if not, then he is a "goat." Because those judged to be sheep are called "the righteous" (v. 37), and because these not only enter the millennial kingdom but also "life eternal" (v. 46), the passing of this simple test must be indicative of a changed heart as well. Only those with changed hearts, having been converted to true faith in Christ, are spoken of elsewhere in Scripture as qualifying for heaven.

That such a test should give this more basic indication is not difficult to understand, in the light of the time involved. During the preceding tribulation period, when the Antichrist will have been venting his hatred against the Jews, any person, other than one who has exercised true faith in Christ, will not care to show himself friendly toward the Jews. It will be too unpopular and even potentially dangerous. When the test reveals one who has befriended the Jews, then it will reveal one who also has placed courageous faith in Christ.

b. Daniel 12:11. The second passage is Daniel 12:11, which seems to indicate the duration of time involved in this period of judging, whether in respect to returning Jews or these Gentiles. The verse reads, "And from the time that the daily sacrifice shall be taken away and the abomination that maketh desolate set up, there shall be a thousand two hundred and ninety days." Note that the figure used, 1,290 days, is thirty days longer than the last half of the tribulation period. The shorter figure, 1,260 days, has been noted in prior discussions, and, in fact, is presented in this same context by the formula, "time, times, and an half"

(v. 7).[7] What is the significance of the extra thirty days? The answer which fits all factors best is that this is the period of time during which these judgments are carried out. A thirty-day period seems appropriate for the two judgments, and it is clear, from the passages noted above, that both judgments do occur at this general time.

In passing, it may be noted that, since these two numbers, 1,260 and 1,290, are used in comparison with each other in the general passage, both must be intended specifically. This indicates, among other things, that the days between the Antichrist's breaking of his treaty with Israel until his defeat by Christ, must be exactly 1,260 days to the day. Therefore, anyone living during the tribulation period who is aware of this should be able to predict the very day of Christ's glorious appearance. [8]

4. *The resurrection of Old Testament and tribulation saints*

Sometime between this exact close of the tribulation and the beginning of the millennial age, another resurrection of saints will occur. This will be a resurrection both of tribulation saints, whether Jews or Gentiles, who have died during the tribulation period, and also of Old Testament saints. Again two passages call for discussion.

a. Revelation 20:4-6. The principal passage is Revelation 20:4-6, which speaks of this resurrection as the "first resurrection" (vv. 5, 6). The question arises as to how this occasion can be called "first" when the resurrection of church saints will have transpired seven years earlier. The answer is that the term "first" is used more to characterize the occasion as to kind, namely a resurrection of the righteous, than as to number in sequence. This idea makes the resurrection of the wicked, which does not occur until after the millennium, the second resurrection, corresponding in name to the "second death," as noted in Revelation 20:6, 14. The term "second" here again carries a connotation basically in respect to kind, rather than sequence. It refers to that kind of death which is eternal in duration.

---

[7] Seen elsewhere to mean 1,260 days; see chapter 6, p. 100.

[8] This fact has a bearing on an argument used in chapter 5, pp. 80, 81, that the rapture cannot occur at the close of the tribulation. If it could, then people could predict the time of the rapture exactly, and numerous passages speak of it as coming by surprise, as a thief in the night.

Actually, there are other occasions of the "first resurrection" than the two just noted. One occurred at the time when Jesus died. At that time, a large number of saints were resurrected, so that they might walk for a time in Jerusalem as living credentials of the authenticity of Christ's resurrection (Matt. 27: 52, 53). It is commonly accepted that these were later taken directly to heaven with glorified bodies. Another resurrection will occur when the "two witnesses," discussed in the previous chapter,[9] will arise from the streets of Jerusalem and be taken to glory. And still a third will occur when millennial saints will rise at the close of the thousand-year period.[10]

The thought of Revelation 20:4-6 is that those who have been "beheaded for the witness of Jesus" during the tribulation time, and have not "worshipped the beast" nor received his "mark upon their foreheads," will be raised again to live and reign "with Christ a thousand years." Verse 6 ascribes blessedness and holiness to these raised ones, saying that the "second death" will have no power over them, to make them experience the torment of eternal hell. The verse also repeats the statement that they will reign with Christ for a thousand years.

b. Daniel 12:2. The other passage is Daniel 12:2. The resurrection of which this verse speaks must be the same one, for it too follows directly after the tribulation period. The tribulation period is the subject of both the verse immediately preceding and the entire last section of Daniel 11. When the verse speaks, then, of "many of them that sleep in the dust" awaking, it speaks first of those who have lived and died during the seven-year period.[11]

From this verse alone, one would not recognize that it is speaking also of saints who lived and died during Old Testament time, but a comparison with Daniel 12:13 shows that it must be. In this closing verse of the chapter, Daniel is told by God to rest

---

[9] See chapter 7, pp. 130-133. Also see chapter 3, pp. 44-46, for further discussion of these resurrections.

[10] Though no Scripture portion can be cited as evidence of this resurrection, its reality follows by force of logic, as noted also in chapter 3.

[11] The following translation shows that the verse need not be taken to mean that both righteous and wicked are raised at this time: "And many that sleep in the dusty ground shall awake; these to everlasting life and others [later on] to everlasting shame and contempt." Also Revelation 20:5 states definitely that "the rest of the dead lived not again until the thousand years were finished."

content with what he then knows in respect to the last days; he should do this until the last days would actually come, for at that time he would "stand in [his] lot at the end of the days." In view of the context, the time in reference must be the close of the tribulation, which means that Daniel is promised a resurrection at that time, when he would inherit his "lot." If Daniel is to be raised at this time, logic says that other Old Testament saints will be as well.

A further reason for placing the resurrection of Old Testament saints here, rather than at the rapture of the church, follows from the general characterization of the tribulation period. This period will have more in common with Old Testament time than the church age preceding. In the church age today, Jews who turn to Christ are made one with Gentiles in the unified body of Christ. Jews of the tribulation period, however, who turn to Christ, will do so as members of the Jewish nation, quite as in Old Testament time. Also, as has been noted, Gentiles will be judged at the close of the period on the basis of their manner of treatment of Jews during the time, thus distinguishing them further from Jews. Therefore, to have both Old Testament and tribulation Jews raised at this same posttribulational moment would group together saints who had a similar background.

This is not to say that only Jews will be involved in this time of resurrection. The stress in Daniel 12:2 is clearly on Jews, for their time of trouble during the tribulation has been the subject of the preceding discussion, but nothing in the verse or context precludes that Gentiles will have a part. It could be presumed, rather, that they will, whether they are Gentiles of Old Testament time or the tribulation period; the former passage noticed, Revelation 20:4-6, calls quite clearly for this to be the case.

5. *The binding of Satan*

Another event which will occur prior to the inauguration of the millennial age is the binding of Satan. During the present age, Satan has freedom to move about as he wishes, promoting his interests and hindering the program of God. This manner of freedom is out of keeping with the idea of the millennium, however. The millennium will be characterized by truth and righteousness, when the "earth shall be full of the knowledge of the LORD, as the waters cover the sea" (Isa. 11:9). The fact of Satan's binding before the millennium begins is presented in Revelation 20:1-3.

The passage speaks of an angel coming down from heaven, with a key to the "bottomless pit" (Greek, *abussou,* "abyss") and a "great chain in his hand." With the latter the angel binds Satan, called here by four terms, "dragon," "serpent," "Devil," and "Satan," apparently as a way of making a positive identification. The angel then casts him into the "bottomless pit," where he is kept securely for one thousand years, the duration of the millennium. At the end of the time, Satan is let loose for "a little season," when he goes forth again to "deceive the nations" (Rev. 20:8). He is somewhat successful at first, being able to gather an army to move against the forces of God. However, fire is sent from God, the army is devoured, and Satan himself is cast into "the lake of fire and brimstone, where the beast and the false prophet are" (Rev. 20:10).

The extent of Satan's influence in the world today is little recognized. Though he is himself not omnipresent, he has hosts of demons who stand ready to serve him. Either directly, or through these helpers, he is able to bring enormous influence on the course of world affairs. Paul realized this and warned the Ephesians accordingly, saying, "For we wrestle not against flesh and blood, but against principalities, against powers, against the rulers of the darkness of this world, against spiritual wickedness in high places" (6:12). It is in recognition of this fact that God confines Satan and his host during the thousand years of the millennium.

Satan will experience an enormous change when he is forced to leave the freedom he enjoyed during the tribulation period and come to this complete confinement of the millennium. During the seven-year period, he will witness his plans and goals being achieved on every hand, as he wields extensive control over the Antichrist and those who assist him. During the thousand-year period, however, he will see only the plans and goals of Christ being brought to pass, as he remains imprisoned in chains.

6. *Establishment of the kingdom*

The last event to be effected during the intervening period is the actual establishment of the millennial reign of Christ. Some matters will call for attention, that this government might become a reality. For instance, an organization will have to be brought to existence. Appointments of personnel will have to be made to fill posts of responsibility. Those selected to fill these posts will be glorified saints, whether of the church (2 Tim. 2:12) or of the tribulation or of Old Testament time (Rev. 20:4). Also, the boundaries of Israel will have to be set. God indicated to Abraham that his seed would rule from the "river of Egypt unto the great river, the river Euphrates" (Gen. 15:18). This has never been achieved in history, although David came the nearest; [12] this means that it will have to be during the millennium, if God's sure word is to be kept. This establishment of boundary will not be difficult at the time, for all the world will lay open for the dictates of Him who has just annihilated the army of the prior ruler.

The amount of time required to effect these matters may be set forth by another chronological indication in Daniel 12. We have noted that the 1,290 days of verse 11 may refer to the additional time necessary, beyond the 1,260 days of the last half of the tribulation, to effect the judgments of both the Jews and Gentiles. But, in the following verse, another figure of 1,335 days is presented. This means that, not only does something occur at the 1,290th day, but also at the 1,335th. The use of the word "blessed" at the beginning of the verse may provide a clue as to what that something is. The word suggests an event wonderful in nature; and what could be more wonderful than the beginning of the millennial reign? This, indeed, may be the significance of the figure. Forty-five days after the conclusion of the judgments, or seventy-five days after the defeat of the Antichrist, the inauguration of the millennium may well be the event which will transpire. If so, the time required to establish the kingdom, including organization, appointments, and setting boundary, will be forty-five days. It may be that the resurrection of saints, as well as the binding of Satan, will occur during these same forty-five days. The total time, then, for both the judgments and the kingdom establishment would be seventy-five days.

---

[12] David's control, however, was not complete between the river of Egypt and the Euphrates. In the region to the north, of which Hamath was capital, for instance, the ruler only recognized David's sovereignty by homage and tribute, but continued to control his own country (2 Sam. 8:9-11; 1 Chron. 18:9-11).

Questions for Review

1. Summarize what Zechariah 14:3, 4 teaches regarding Christ's coming in power.
2. Summarize what Matthew 24:27-30 teaches regarding this occasion.
3. What main points regarding this coming are made in Revelation 19:11-16?
4. What vivid picture is presented in Revelation 19:17, 18?
5. What is the end of the Antichrist and the False Prophet? Of their army?
6. State in your own words the nine points of summary given regarding this glorious coming of Christ.
7. List some passages of Scripture which state that Jews in Israel will accept Christ as their Messiah at this time of coming.
8. What does Ezekiel 20:33-38 teach about a judgment of Jews at this time?
9. What is the purpose of the judgment of Gentiles which occurs at this time?
10. What is the test employed at this time of judgment?
11. What may be the significance of the figure 1,290 given in Daniel 12:11?
12. What is the significance of the term "first resurrection" used in Revelation 20:5, 6?
13. What reasons may be given for believing that Old Testament saints are raised at the close of the tribulation week, rather than at the rapture?
14. Will any Gentiles be raised at this posttribulation occasion?
15. What is the rationale for Satan being bound during the millennium, when he is not today?
16. What does Satan do as soon as he is loosed again?
17. What are some of the things that will need to be done in setting up the millennial kingdom?
18. What may be the significance of the figure 1,335 given in Daniel 12:12?

9

The
Millennium

Men have long dreamed of a utopia on earth. The thinking usually has been that this would be achieved through the improved knowledge and technology of man himself. Even a cursory reading of daily newspapers and periodicals, however, shows that this will not happen. But there will indeed be a day when utopian conditions will exist. This will be the day when God brings them about, the day of the millennium, when Christ will reign as King of all the world. The Scriptures have much to say about this future period. It is our task now to consider numerous passages, to see what the principal features of that wonderful day will be.

A. Characteristics

An earlier chapter has set the historical background of the day. It will come when Satan's false world ruler, the Antichrist, has been deposed and when proper designation of those to enter the glorious period has been made. A brief time will be used to establish the workings of the new government, and then will come the inauguration of the perfect King. We will first note the principal characteristics of the period.

1. *Recognition of God's authority*

To help identify and understand these characteristics, we should first note the basic idea of the period. God has a purpose in all that He does, and His plan for the millennium is no exception. The basic idea is to have a period when God's authority will be recognized in all the earth. God's universal kingdom has been in effect, but His highest creation, free moral man, has refused to render obedience. Because of Christ's gracious provision of salvation at His first coming, individual persons have bowed, making God's rule a reality in their own hearts; but mankind at large has not given Him due recognition. For this reason the great potential blessings of God's creation have not been realized. The sinfulness of man has kept the world from seeing in their fulness the beautiful, wonderful conditions which God's handiwork had promised.

Something of what might have been, had sin not entered the scene, may be drawn from the idyllic situation of Adam and Eve, as they were in the Garden of Eden. The physical conditions they enjoyed were clearly to their greatest advantage. Also, the sense of peace and rest they knew has probably not been experienced since. Most of all, there was the closeness of fellowship with God, in which direct communication between God and man occurred with some frequency. When sin entered, however, all changed. Man became estranged from God, and strife became the rule of the day. Governments came into existence to control strife, but, being led by sinful men, they were corrupt. Man fought with man, communities with communities, and nations with nations. Suffering, hardships, disease, famine, injustice, and loss of fellowship with God developed on every hand. With all this God was not pleased. His perfect creation held potential for so much more. As long as sin continued to be in command, however, matters could only continue in this way.

But God will not permit this situation always to exist. He will have His authority recognized. His kingdom will come, not only in the hearts of individuals but in all the world. Time will not cease nor the eternal state begin without His masterpiece of creation witnessing His will being observed and the great promises fulfilled. This will come to pass under the rule of the perfect King, Christ Himself. What might have been, will be. God will see His handiwork accomplish that for which He made it, and man will have an existence of peace and happiness to meet his fondest desire.

A parallel fulfillment will be seen in connection with God's chosen people, the Jews. God molded them into a nation in Old Testament days, that they might be God's kingdom in the world. Accordingly, when they entered their land of promise, they had a glorious future awaiting them, if they would only do the will of God. This is outlined clearly, for example, in Deuteronomy 28:1-14, where God states that they would become the leading people of the world, if they would follow Him. He would set them "on high above all nations of the earth" (v. 1), so that they would be "above only, and . . . not be beneath," being "the head, and not the tail" (v. 13). This did not occur, however, because the people did not meet the condition of obedience. It became necessary, instead, for God to permit neighboring nations to impose servitude on His people as a means of discipline.

To Abraham, God had promised the land "from the river of Egypt unto the great river, the river Euphrates (Gen. 15:18), but this promise was never fulfilled. Land was given, but never that much — not even in the day of David and Solomon, when the boundaries extended furthest. God also had promised Abraham that in him should "all families of the earth be blessed" (Gen. 12:3). This has occurred in a spiritual way, since Christ came of the seed of Abraham; but it has not happened in a physical way, and that thought also was intended. The great truth of the millennium is that all these promises will be fulfilled, because then true allegiance will be rendered to the King. Israel will become the leading nation of the world, her borders will stretch from Egypt to the Euphrates, and she will be the influence and world-wide blessing predicted.

It should be recognized that these matters will be accomplished without great change in the normal conditions of human life. Basic structures and institutions of society will probably continue. Life styles and patterns, with individuals manifesting their distinct personalities, will remain. People will eat, sleep, earn a living, marry, have children, and finally die. There will be cities, farms, schools, industries, and stores. The difference will consist in the presence of proper, enjoyable relationships among people and especially toward God. Righteousness will prevail, and people will think and converse about God. Zechariah writes that even such a relatively insignificant item as "the bells on the horses" will carry the words, "HOLINESS UNTO THE LORD" (14:20).

2. *Ideals realized*

In nobler moments, people have ideals in their minds which they would like to see realized. The millennium will see them brought to fruition. One of the highest ideals is justice. When innocent people suffer and criminals go free, the hearts of people cry out for justice. Christ's rule will be characterized by perfect justice. Jeremiah tells of the day in these words: "A King shall reign and prosper, and shall execute judgment and justice in the earth" (23:5). Isaiah speaks also of the day, as he states, "But with righteousness shall he judge the poor, and reprove with equity for the meek of the earth" (11:4). Isaiah also gives the reason why Christ will be able to dispense justice of this kind: "He shall not judge after the sight of his eyes, neither reprove after the hearing of his ears" (11:3). Christ will make sure that His just decisions are effected, because "he shall smite the earth with the rod of his mouth, and with the breath of his lips shall he slay the wicked" (11:4). No rebellion will be permitted and no bribes will be accepted. Every person will receive his just due.

Not only will Christ dispense justice to others, but He will rule in perfect righteousness Himself. One of the problems in government today is the existence of unrighteous actions. A common term of the day is "credibility gap," and the reason is that public personnel have demonstrated a conduct which makes people suspicious. Graft, under-the-table trades, favoritism to people of power and wealth — all are prevalent today. But this will not be true under the rule of Christ. Again it is Isaiah who writes, "Righteousness shall be the girdle of his loins" (11:5). A striking passage is found in Psalm 45:6, 7: "Thy throne, O God, is for ever and ever: the sceptre of thy kingdom is a right sceptre. Thou lovest righteousness and hatest wickedness: therefore God, thy God, hath anointed thee with the oil of gladness above thy fellows." No reason will exist for a credibility gap during the millennium.

Involved in the concept of righteousness, is the concept of truth. Truth will be held in high regard during the millennium. Zechariah writes of the day when he says that "Jerusalem shall be called a city of truth" (8:3). Satan has been the father of lies from the beginning (John 8:44), and governments through all of history have followed his lead. But Christ, who is "the truth" (John 14:6), will provide truthful government in all respects.

Still another area of high ideals includes mercy and tenderness. The world knows little of either. So often governments are cold and hard, especially toward the unimportant person. But a watchword of Christianity is an attitude of mercy and tenderness, and this will be carried out in the world at large when Christ rules. Isaiah makes this clear, as he speaks also of other matters already noted: "And in mercy shall the throne be established: and he shall sit upon it in truth in the tabernacle of David, judging, and seeking judgment and hasting righteousness" (16:5). Isaiah further states that this one, who will rule so effectively, shall at the same time "feed his flock like a shepherd: he shall gather the lambs with his arm, and carry them in his bosom, and shall gently lead those that are with young" (40:11). To achieve a balance between mercy on the one hand and justice on the other is not easy. Good rulers have tried, but their lack of success has been more than apparent. The perfect harmony will be found and maintained by Christ.

3. *Blessings enjoyed*

Closely related to the thought of ideals realized is that of blessings enjoyed. The millennium will witness great blessings from God. Many of these will be the result of the ideals being realized. That is, because Christ's government will operate with its high principles, people will reap wonderful benefits. They will be the recipients of just decisions, will profit from the true and righteous conduct exhibited, and will respond to the merciful and tender ministrations extended. Also, righteous conduct in government will bring a similar response on the part of people. Psalm 72:7 states that in that coming day "shall the righteous flourish; and abundance of peace so long as the moon endureth."

a. An outpouring of the Holy Spirit. One highly significant area of blessing will be the outpouring of the Holy Spirit in the lives of people. Ezekiel speaks of the day as he depicts God saying, "And I will put my spirit within you, and cause you to walk in my statutes" (36:27). Joel 2:28, 29 is a key passage; God declares, "I will pour out my spirit upon all flesh; and your sons and your daughters shall prophesy, your old men shall dream dreams, your young men shall see visions: and also upon the servants and upon the handmaids in those days will I pour out my spirit." A partial fulfillment of this came at Pentecost (Acts 2:16-18). The greater fulfillment, however, is to come during the millennium, as shown by following verses in Joel 2. These speak of the sun being "turned into darkness and the moon into blood, before the great and terrible day of the LORD come" (v. 31). This will be the day when deliverance will be effected for those "in mount Zion and in Jerusalem" (v. 32). These events will transpire just preceding the millennium, as previous discussions have shown.

One major result of this outpouring of the Holy Spirit will be widespread salvation. People will place saving faith in Christ their King. The descendants of those who inherit the kingdom, will need to exercise this faith. The first inhabitants will already be saved, even before the kingdom's inauguration. Their children, however, will still be born in sin. The unrestricted presence of the Holy Spirit will lead them to trust Christ. Probably it will be as natural and easy to do this then as now it seemingly is difficult to do so. Isaiah sees himself living in that day, as he writes, "He hath clothed me with the garments of salvation, he hath covered me with the robe of righteousness" (61:10). Again, he declares that in that day the very walls of Jerusalem will be called "salvation" (60:18). Then men with joy shall "draw water out of the wells of salvation" (12:3).

Another significant result of the outpouring of the Holy Spirit will be the evidence of God's abundant grace. God will manifest His grace in numerous ways, and people will be aware of it and give thanksgiving accordingly. Zechariah declares that in that day God will "pour upon the house of David . . . the spirit of grace" (12:10). Psalm 45 says of Christ the King, "Grace is poured into thy lips" (v. 2).

A third result will be that people will be led to live righteous lives. It has been noted that Christ will rule righteously. But also people at large will be led to follow His example, as the Holy Spirit prompts and inspires to that end. Ezekiel says directly that as a result of God putting His spirit within the people of the day, they will walk in His statutes and keep His judgments (36:27). This will bring the people to remember their "own evil ways, and [their] doings that were not good" (36:31). Zephaniah describes the result with these words, "The remnant of Israel shall not do iniquity, nor speak lies; neither shall a deceitful tongue be found in their mouth: for they shall feed and lie down, and none shall make them afraid" (3:13).

b. A state of peace. Another area of blessing will be the existence of a wondrous peace. There will be no war during the millennium. War has been the scourge of history, but this will not be true then. Isaiah states: "Of the increase of his government and peace there shall be no end" (9:7). Micah specifically declares of that day: "They shall beat their swords into plow-shares, and their spears into pruninghooks: nations shall not lift up a sword against nation, neither shall they learn war any more" (4:3). Hosea speaks of that time when he writes, "In that day . . . I will break the bow and the sword and the battle out of the earth, and will make them to lie down safely " (2:18). A by-product of this peace will be the absence of fear. Micah states, "But they shall sit every man under his vine and under his fig tree; and none shall make them afraid" (4:4).

   c. Observance of social justice. A further area of blessing concerns social justice. For instance, people will be able to enjoy what they earn for themselves, without others taking it from them. Writes Isaiah, "And they shall build houses, and inhabit them; and they shall plant vineyards, and eat the fruit of them. They shall not build, and another inhabit; they shall not plant, and another eat" (65:21, 22). The poor will not be exploited by the rich. The psalmist speaks of the day, saying, "He shall judge the poor of the people, he shall save the children of the needy, and shall break in pieces the oppressor" (Ps. 72:4; cf. vv. 12-14). The need of the individual, even if he has little strength or talent, will not be lost in the interest of society, for "a bruised reed shall he not break, and the smoking flax shall he not quench"; but instead Christ will "bring forth judgment unto truth" (Isa. 42:3).

   d. Physical benefits. Still another area of blessing involves the physical world. For one thing, shortage of water will not be a problem, as it has been for the Palestine area all through history. Isaiah prophesied, "In the wilderness shall waters break out, and streams in the desert. And the parched ground shall become a pool, and the thirsty land springs of water" (35:6, 7; cf. Ezek. 34:26; Joel 2:21-24). Abundant rainfall, in turn, will bring ex-cellent crops. Isaiah tells of regions which formerly knew only "thorns and briers" being made "a fruitful field" (32:13-15); the desert will then "blossom as the rose" (35:1; cf. Ezek. 36:4-11). Isaiah refers also to changes in animal nature, as he says, "The wolf also shall dwell with the lamb, and the leopard shall lie down with the kid; and the calf and the young lion and the fatling together; and a little child shall lead them" (Isa. 11:6; cf. 7, 8). Hosea has the same thought in mind as he writes of the safety that men will then feel in respect to animals, "And in that day will I make a covenant for them with the beasts of the field, . . . and will make them to lie down safely" (2:18; Ezek. 34:25).

A few passages indicate that physical deformity and disease will be rectified. Isaiah writes, "Then the eyes of the blind shall be opened, and the ears of the deaf shall be unstopped. Then shall the lame man leap as an hart, and the tongue of the dumb sing" (35:5, 6). Again, he states, "The inhabitant shall not say, I am sick" (33:24), suggesting that disease will be virtually unknown. This in turn will result in long life; Isaiah further writes, "There shall be no more thence an infant of days, nor an old man that hath not filled his days: for the child shall die an hundred years old" (65:20; cf. vv. 21, 22).

e. A sense of well-being. A last area of blessing is really the result of the others: a sense of joy and well-being among people generally. Numerous passages might be cited. Isaiah, for instance, states, "The Lord GOD will wipe away tears from off all faces; . . . we will be glad and rejoice in his salvation" (25:8, 9); "Ye shall have a song, as in the night . . . and gladness of heart" (30:29); "Whereas thou hast been forsaken and hated, . . . I will make thee an eternal excellency, a joy of many generations" (60:15); "Everlasting joy shall be unto them" (61:7). Jeremiah 30:19 says, "Out of them shall proceed thanksgiving and the voice of them that make merry."

4. Duration of the millennium

a. Continues for thousand years. The duration of the millennium is clearly established in Revelation 20:1-7 as one thousand years. Though this figure is used in Scripture only here, its manner of usage makes the literal intention unmistakable. It is mentioned no less than six times, and each time it is in reference to a distinct feature of the period. The force of this is to say, in six different ways, that the duration will indeed be of this length. In verse 2, it refers to the length of time Satan will be bound; in verse 3, to the time nations will not be deceived by him; in verse 4, to the time martyred saints will reign with Christ; in verse 5, to the time during which the "rest of the dead" (i.e., the wicked dead) will wait until their resurrection; in verse 6, to the time those who rise in the first resurrection will reign with Christ; and in verse 7, to the time which will elapse before Satan will again be loosed from his confinement in the bottomless pit.

Adherents of both amillennialism and postmillennialism deny the literalness of this reference. They hold that the thousand years are to be understood symbolically, with most taking them to refer merely to an indefinite, long period of time. These same scholars, however, believe that other elements from the passage are to be taken literally, such as the resurrections mentioned, Satan, heaven, the angel, and the binding or restraining of Satan. The question becomes pertinent, then, as to the reason for making a distinction with the thousand years. The writings of the early church fathers show that it was interpreted literally by those near to the Apostles, and also later by the church in general for at least three hundred years.

b. Continues for all eternity. It should also be noted that a sense exists in which Christ's kingdom will last actually for all eternity. The earthly aspect of the kingdom, with Christ ruling out of Jerusalem, will last only the limited time. But there will be a continuation of the rule, which will have no end. At the conclusion of the thousand years, there will be a merging of the earthly form of the kingdom into God's eternal rule. At that time, Christ will deliver up "the kingdom to God, even the Father," and there will be an adjustment of its character and dimensions to eternal proportions rather than temporal (cf. 1 Cor. 15:24-28).

Numerous Scripture passages, which speak of the kingdom, carry their primary reference to the eternal aspect, rather than the temporal (see, for example, 2 Sam. 7:16; Ps. 45:6). In determining which passages do this, a word of caution is called for. The English translation "forever" is not a sure indication. This translation represents the Hebrew *'olam,* which can mean either "eternity" or "long time." In several instances where the King James Version renders it "forever," it is better taken as "long time." The context must determine which is preferable. A general rule to follow is to note the character of the kingdom as indicated in the context. If it is of an earthly nature, then reference should be understood to be to the temporal aspect, and the translation should be "long time." If the thought is centered in continuity of rule, without earthly features being involved, then reference is to the eternal espect, and the translation should be "forever" or "eternity."

B. Government

One of the basic questions regarding the millennium is the nature of the government which will be inaugurated. What will it be like? How will it operate? Who will comprise its personnel? The Scriptures have much to say concerning these matters.

1. *Christ will be King*

The first point to notice is that Christ will serve as the supreme, absolute Ruler. This was foretold to Mary by the angel Gabriel, when announcing the birth of Jesus: "The Lord God shall give unto him the throne of his father David: and he shall reign over the house of Jacob for ever" (Luke 1:32, 33). This was announced long before in Psalm 2:6, as God declares, in the face of implied opposition from earthly kings, "Yet have I set my king upon my holy hill of Zion." Isaiah prophesied, "And the government shall be upon his shoulder. Of the increase of his government and peace there shall be no end" (9:6, 7). In Revelation 19:16, as Christ comes in power to defeat the Antichrist and his army, the name ascribed to Him is "KING OF KINGS, AND LORD OF LORDS." [1] Christ, indeed, must be the King, for only then could the conditions already noticed be met. He alone qualifies as the perfect King.

a. Both God and man. As the supreme Ruler, Christ will be both God and man in one Person, even as when He was on earth the first time. This dual relationship of the divine and human did not cease at the Ascension. Christ continues in this twofold form today and will return as such. One may safely anticipate that in His role as King He will act principally out of His human nature, just as at His first coming. Isaiah describes Him as King, using language which indicates this. "And there shall come forth a rod out of the stem of Jesse, and a branch shall grow out of his roots: And the spirit of the LORD shall rest upon him, the spirit of wisdom and understanding, the spirit of counsel and might, the spirit of knowledge and of the fear of the LORD" (11:1, 2). He will no doubt act quite as other kings, so far as the mechanics of government are concerned. At the same time, there is no reason why He should find it necessary to limit Himself to merely human attributes. Rather, He will probably find it appropriate to employ His divine abilities as well, as the case may call for them. His work as man's substitute was finished at the cross, which leaves no requirement for the extreme self-limitation to which He submitted at His first coming.

b. The perfect Sovereign. Serving as supreme Ruler, Christ will be the perfect, ideal Sovereign. History has never seen one,

---

[1] Cf. Isa. 2:1-4; 11:1-10; 24:23; 40:10, 11; Dan. 2:44; 7:13, 14, 27; Micah 4:1-8; Zech. 14:9, 16, 17.

but Christ will fill this role completely. He will have the necessary knowledge, wisdom, attitude, integrity, and, above all, freedom from sin which can and will make this possible. Because of the perfect quality of the rule, His government will be autocratic (Ps. 2:9; 72:9-11; Isa. 11:4). Today, when only sinful men exist to rule, the type of government which contributes most to the well-being of people is democratic. A democracy, however, is not the perfect form of government, as history clearly testifies. An autocracy is less costly and more efficient. But to make an autocracy work for the true good of people, the supreme ruler must be a perfect man, without sin. Christ will be this One.

c. The "David" passages. An interesting question concerns passages which speak of "David" ruling during the millennium. These passages are Jeremiah 30:9; Ezekiel 34:23, 24; 37:24, 25; and Hosea 3:5. What relation exists between the "David" thus mentioned and Christ? Is "David" here another name for Christ, or is the name a reference specifically to David, who would, then, be in his resurrected form? The question is not easy to answer. [2]

Both Walvoord and Pentecost [3] favor the view that this person will be the resurrected David. The latter argues as follows:

> The objections to this view [that this "David" is Christ] arise (1) from the fact that Christ is never called David in the Scriptures. He is called the Branch unto David (Jer. 23: 5), Son of David (15 times), Seed of David (John 7:42; Rom. 1:3; 2 Tim. 2:8), Root of David (Rev. 5:5), and Root and Offspring of David (Rev. 22:16), but never David. (2) The appellation "my servant, David" is used repeatedly for the historical David. (3) In Hosea 3:5; Ezekiel 37: 21-25; 34:24; Jeremiah 30:9 and Isaiah 55:4 Jehovah is clearly distinguished from David. If in these passages David typically referred to Christ, no distinction could be made,

---

[2] A third view is also held; namely, that this "David" is a son of David, other than Christ, who will sit on the throne. A major argument is taken from identifying with "David" a "prince," mentioned frequently by Ezekiel (e.g., 44:3; 45:7, 8, 9, 16, 17, 22, etc.). This "prince" could not be Christ Himself, for he is said to present offerings for himself (46:2). This identification is not likely, however. Also, if these "David" passages call for another than David himself, Christ is surely the likely one, otherwise Christ is made less than the complete fulfillment of the Davidic promises.

[3] John F. Walvoord, *The Millennial Kingdom,* pp. 300, 301; J. Dwight Pentecost, *Things To Come,* pp. 498-501.

nor would one need be so carefully drawn. (4) There are statements concerning this prince which preclude the application of the title to Christ. In Ezekiel 45:22 the prince is said to offer a sin offering for himself. Even if these are memorial sacrifices, as shall be shown, Christ could not offer a memorial sacrifice for His own sin, since He was sinless. In Ezekiel 46:2 the prince is engaged in acts of worship. Christ receives worship in the millennium, but does not engage in acts of worship. In Ezekiel 46:16 the prince has sons and divides an inheritance with them. Such could not be done by Christ. For these reasons it seems that the prince referred to as David could not be Christ. [4]

In my judgment, however, these arguments are not altogether convincing. In respect to the first reason, one is minded to say that, though Christ is more often called by such relationships to David, as indicated, still the very passages in view may be the places where He is called David. For Him to be designated in this manner would not be greatly different from Malachi's reference to Elijah, predicting that he would come before "the great and dreadful day of the LORD" (Mal. 4:5). Pentecost himself agrees that this reference is not to Elijah himself, but to one who would minister "in the spirit and power of Elijah." [5] In other words, Elijah's name is used metaphorically. The same could be true of this reference to David; it could be a metaphorical way of referring to Christ, who would rule on Israel's throne after the pattern of the historical David.

Regarding the second reason, no disagreement can be made with Pentecost's assertion, but one wonders at its strength. The phrase, "my servant, David," is used, indeed, as the argument implies, in two of the pertinent passages here involved (Ezek. 34: 23, 24; 37:24, 25), but this serves merely to identify more specifically the person of history who is metaphorically used to refer to Christ.

In respect to the third reason, the distinction between Jehovah and Christ here noted is used in other millennial passages, so why not here? For instance, in Psalm 2:6-9 Jehovah sets Christ in His kingdom, calls Him His Son, tells Him to ask and He will give Him the heathen for His inheritance, etc. (cf. Heb. 1:5-9).

[4] J. Dwight Pentecost, Things To Come, p. 499. Used by permission.
[5] See Things To Come, pp. 309-313, for discussion.

Concerning the fourth reason, the "prince" in reference in Ezekiel 45:22 and 46:2, 16 need not be this "David." Even if he were the historical David, as Pentecost believes, it is not clear why he would offer a "sin offering for himself," for David then will be in resurrected form, and not subject to sin any longer. The action would be out of place for him as well as for Christ. This "prince" could well be a chief officer under Christ, who would be appointed from people then alive, who, then, would be subject to sinning. Such a one would also need to engage in acts of worship and could have sons, as Ezekiel indicates.

A later statement of Pentecost [6] that "resurrected saints are to have positions of responsibility in the millennium" is very true, and the statement does lend some credence to this view. David, of course, will be among such resurrected saints, and it is logical to think that his assignment would be in respect to Israel. If so, one could expect that it would be a high assignment. This would fit the idea that he could be such a vice-regent under Christ, as this view sets forth (see Matt. 8:11).

At the same time, the thought that the particular references to David in these "David" passages could be to the David of history, ruling only in the capacity of a vice-regent, is not easy to accept. The context of the references is not in keeping with the idea merely of vice-regency, but to the head office, the kingship. And other passages clearly indicate who that head One will be — Christ Himself. The angel Gabriel told Mary, speaking of her son to be born, "The Lord God shall give unto him the throne of his father David: and he shall reign over the house of Jacob" (Luke 1:32, 33; cf. Isa. 9:6, 7).

2. *King over Israel*

a. The fact. Not only will Christ's millennial kingship include His rule over Israel as a nation, but this nation will claim a primary place in His attention. He will be especially Israel's King. Writes Jeremiah, "Behold, the days come, saith the LORD, that I will raise unto David a righteous Branch, and a King shall reign and prosper, . . . and this is his name whereby he shall be called, THE LORD OUR RIGHTEOUSNESS" (23:5, 6). Micah talks about a day when Israel shall be great in strength and then gives the reason: "The LORD shall reign over them in mount Zion"

---

[6] *Things To Come,* p. 500.

(4:7). Isaiah also speaks of unusual days for the land "when the LORD of hosts shall reign in mount Zion, and in Jerusalem, and before his ancients gloriously" (24:23).

b. Judah and Israel united. Under Christ's rule, there will be no division to the land, as there was after the reign of Solomon. Judah and Israel will exist as one united nation. This is the thought of Ezekiel 37:15-22, where the prophet is told by God to join two sticks and make them one. The point is brought out in verse 22: "And I will make them one nation in the land upon the mountains of Israel; and one king shall be king to them all; and they shall be no more two nations, neither shall they be divided into two kingdoms any more at all." Jeremiah writes similarly, "In those days the house of Judah shall walk with the house of Israel, and they shall come together out of the land of the north to the land that I have given for an inheritance unto your fathers" (3:18; cf. 33:14; Hosea 1:11).

c. A true people of God. Great blessing from God will flow on the people, because they will be a true people of God. Sin withheld blessing in Old Testament days (Deut. 28:15-68). But righteousness will prevail during the millennium. Jeremiah depicts God saying, "And I will give them an heart to know me, that I am the LORD: and they shall be my people, and I will be their God: for they shall return unto me with their whole heart" (24:7). Ezekiel says of the day, "Neither shall they defile themselves any more with their idols, nor with their detestable things, nor with any of their transgressions" (37:23). Hosea says that, as a result, God will "betroth" Israel unto Himself "in righteousness, and in judgment, and in lovingkindness, and in mercies" (2:19; cf. Isa. 4:3, 4; Jer. 33:8; Ezek. 36:25, 26).

d. Admired by Gentiles. Because of sin in Old Testament days, Israel was made a "reproach" to her neighbors, "a scorn and a derision" to those round about, a byword among the heathen, a shaking of the head among the people" (Ps. 44:13, 14). This too will be different during the millennium. Israel then will be admired. Isaiah paints the picture vividly, as he speaks directly to the nation: "The sons also of them that afflicted thee shall come bending unto thee; and all they that despised thee shall bow themselves down at the soles of thy feet; . . . whereas thou hast been forsaken and hated, . . . I will make thee an eternal excellency, a joy of many generations" (60:14, 15). Again he writes, "Ye shall eat the riches of the Gentiles, and in their glory shall ye boast yourselves. For your shame ye shall have double; and for confusion they shall rejoice in their portion" (61:6, 7; cf. 14:1, 2; 49:22, 23; 62:2-5).

e. World center of worship at Jerusalem. As a result of these realities, Jerusalem will become the world center of worship. Isaiah, speaking to Israel, writes that "the LORD shall arise upon thee, and his glory shall be seen upon thee, . . . And the Gentiles shall come to thy light, and kings to the brightness of thy rising" (60:2, 3). He further states that "the sons of strangers shall build up thy walls, and their kings shall minister unto thee" (60:10). Micah is even more explicit:

> But in the last days it shall come to pass, that the mountain of the house of the LORD shall be established in the top of the mountains . . . and people shall flow unto it. And many nations shall come, and say, Come, and let us go up to the mountain of the LORD, and to the house of the God of Jacob; and he will teach us of his ways, and we will walk in his paths: for the law shall go forth of Zion, and the word of the LORD from Jerusalem (4:1, 2; cf. Isa. 61:6; Jer. 3:17; 16:19-21; Mic. 5:7; Zech. 8:23).

3. *King over the Gentiles*

a. The fact. Though Christ will serve as King with special reference to Israel, He will act as King over the rest of the world as well. He will be what Satan's false king, the Antichrist, tried to be. In Psalm 2:8, God the Father bids the Son, "Ask of me, and I shall give thee the heathen for thine inheritance, and the uttermost parts of the earth for thy possession." In Nebuchadnezzar's first recorded dream, "the stone," which symbolized Christ's kingdom, "became a great mountain, and filled the whole earth" (Dan. 2:35). In Daniel's first vision, Christ, as the Son of man, was given "dominion, and glory, and a kingdom, that all people, nations, and languages, should serve him" (Dan. 7:14; cf. v. 27; Ps. 72:8-11; Isa. 2:4; 42:1; Zech. 9:10; 14:9).

b. Gentiles subservient to Israel. The scriptural picture clearly shows that Israel will be the leading nation of the world during the millennium, with Gentiles being subservient. Isaiah writes,

> For the LORD will have mercy on Jacob, . . . and the strangers [Gentiles] shall be joined with them, . . . and the house of Israel shall possess them in the land of the LORD

for servants and handmaids: and they shall take them captives, whose captives they were; and they shall rule over their
oppressors (14:1, 2).

Later he states,

Thus saith the Lord GOD, Behold, I will lift up mine hand
to the Gentiles, and set up my standard to the people: and
they shall bring thy sons in their arms, and thy daughters
shall be carried upon their shoulders. And kings shall be
thy nursing fathers, and their queens thy nursing mothers:
they shall bow down to thee with their face toward the earth,
and lick up the dust of thy feet (49:22, 23; cf. 60:14; 61:
5-9; Zech. 8:22, 23).

The thought is that Israel will be the honored nation of the world,
with other nations giving her due recognition. Because the millennium will be a time of blessing for all, including the Gentiles,
one should not think of the Gentiles rebelling at this. Rather,
with Christ as the all-glorious King over Israel in Jerusalem, they
will find joy in being able to give this recognition. No doubt the
benefits of Christ's perfect rule will be so great and universal
that Gentiles will feel no sense of loss due to the supreme honor
given to Israel.

   c. Gentiles also a true people of God. The Scriptures regularly depict Gentiles, along with the Jews, as being a true people of
God during this time. Isaiah speaks of Egypt, for instance, in
that day, as he states, "And the LORD shall be known to Egypt,
and the Egyptians shall know the LORD in that day, and shall do
sacrifice and oblation; yea, they shall vow a vow unto the LORD,
and perform it" (19:21). Jeremiah writes, "At that time they
shall call Jerusalem the throne of the LORD; and all the nations
shall be gathered unto it, to the name of the LORD, to Jerusalem:
neither shall they walk any more after the imagination of their
evil heart" (3:17; cf. Isa. 61:8, 9; Jer. 16:19-21; Zech. 8:20-22).
This is in keeping with Isaiah's general statement, "The earth
shall be full of the knowledge of the LORD, as the waters cover
the sea" (11:9), and with Daniel's indication that "the saints of
the most High shall . . . possess the kingdom for ever" (7:18;
cf. vv. 22, 27). Both Jews and Gentiles, then, will be people of
God, finding their delight in the great King, Jesus Christ.

   d. Gentile government. The Scriptures say little regarding the mechanics of Gentile rule. Christ will of course be the King, conducting His rule out of Jerusalem. But how the world under His supreme rule will be administered is not clear. It may be that national boundaries will be maintained much like today. Probably the heads of nations will be appointed by, and will report to, the supreme King. One point is sure: whatever the form of administration, it will be for the best because it will be established by Christ Himself.

4. *Glorified saints will rule with Christ*

Another point made clear is that most of those whom Christ appoints to office will be glorified saints, who will be raised from the dead, either before or after the tribulation period. Paul writes to the Corinthians, "Do ye not know that the saints shall judge the world?" (1 Cor. 6:2). He says to Timothy, "If we suffer, we shall also reign with him" (2 Tim. 2:12; cf. Rev. 5:10; 20:4). Speaking more specifically of Israel, Christ tells the disciples, "Ye which have followed me . . . shall sit upon twelve thrones, judging the twelve tribes of Israel" (Matt. 19:28). Glorified saints would have to rule, since they alone would be qualified to officiate, at least in the most important positions. If a sinless King is required to make the utopian conditions of the millennium, then sinless subordinates must be necessary as well. If this were not so, the subordinates could fail in carrying out the King's orders. Key personnel will have to be able to meet the highest standards in performance and moral integrity. Any appointments of non-glorified saints, then, could only be from the choicest of persons and then to offices of lesser importance.

C. Subjects

One meaningful division of subjects over whom Christ will rule has been discussed: the division of Jews in Israel and Gentiles elsewhere. Another division also exists: glorified saints and living saints. This distinction has been involved in prior discussions, but not dealt with as such. As has been seen, glorified saints are those who experience resurrection and the bestowal of glorified bodies. Saints of the present church age will experience this glorification at the rapture, while those of Old Testament time and those who die during the tribulation will receive it at the post-tribulational resurrection. Living saints will be those who live their normal course of life during the millennium. Both groups continue to exist throughout the thousand-year period, and several matters in respect to their interrelation call for attention.

1. *The comparative number of each*

Surprising as it may seem, the number of glorified saints, at the beginning of the millennium, will no doubt be larger than that of living saints. Glorified saints will include all the saved of the church age and of Old Testament time and those who die during the tribulation, a total numbering in the millions. On the other hand, living saints will include only those Gentiles who have passed Christ's test, of having treated the Jews properly, and only those among the Jews who have placed faith in Christ and escaped martyrdom. The Jews alone should number more than a million, however, for one-third of the total population will survive the tribulation (Zech. 13:8, 9), and the population of Jews in Israel today is approaching three million. Also, as has been seen in an earlier chapter, [7] the number of Gentiles who turn to Christ will be considerable. But still the total number will certainly fall well short of the number of glorified saints.

This imbalance can be expected to last for only a short time, however. The number of glorified saints will not change, as the years pass, for they will not marry or have children. The number of living saints, on the other hand, can be expected to grow rapidly. The birth rate will probably be high and the death rate low, under the advantageous conditions enjoyed. Even after only a few generations, living saints could already be a majority, and many generations will pass before the full thousand years are completed. By the time the millennium comes to an end, living saints can be expected to greatly outnumber glorified saints.

2. *Will all glorified saints rule?*

It has been noted that Christ will find His personnel for service mainly from the ranks of glorified saints. How many will be asked to serve? One must be careful in attempting answers where the Scriptures are silent. The passages already noted simply give the general indication that resurrected saints will reign, but without telling how many (Matt. 19:28; 1 Cor. 6:2; 2 Tim. 2:12; Rev. 5:10; 20:4). The most specific indication comes from Matthew 19:28, where Jesus says that the disciples will rule over

---

[7] See chapter 4, p. 72.

the twelve tribes of Israel, apparently one to a tribe; but even this gives very little real help. Logical deduction can be applied, however, which should give some indication. At the beginning of the millennium, when glorified saints outnumber the living, certainly not all will rule. A government can hardly have more rulers than subjects. As the number of living saints increases, however, the need for more rulers will grow; and probably, before the millennium closes, all glorified saints will be needed.

3. *Righteousness among Christ's subjects*

One of the fine, meaningful characteristics of the millennium will be the righteous conduct among people. Instead of cheating, lying, oppression, and malicious gossip one will find fair play, truthfulness, justice, and sympathetic understanding. In the world of today, a person expects to find sin and unrighteousness on every hand. Because this is so, one tends to become hardened to sin and even to take it for granted. God, however, is not pleased with this. The original creation was just and good. Man in his first state was righteous. He became abnormal when he fell into sin. The millennial age will see a return to God's original plan. This will be a most significant change and cause for rejoicing.

This rejoicing will be tempered somewhat, however, by a limited amount of sin existent. Sin will not be nearly as prevalent as today, and it will not be accepted by society nor considered normal. Certainly it will not take the flagrant forms now found. But still it will be present, as several considerations show. First, living saints will not yet have their glorified bodies, which means that their bodies will be subject to passions and lusts. Second, the very fact that Satan will need to be bound indicates that people will still have natures to which he could appeal. Third, Christ is said to rule with a rod of iron (Ps. 2:9), reproving "with equity for the meek of the earth" (Isa. 11:4; cf. Ps. 72: 1-4; Isa. 29:20, 21; 65:20; 66:24; Zech. 14:16-21); this shows that disobedience in some degree will occur. Fourth, that Satan will be able to find sympathizers to form an army at the very close of the age with which to make a final attack on the hosts of Christ (Rev. 20:7-9), indicates that some people will then live who will be openly rebellious against Christ.

This is evidence not only that sin will exist, but that some persons will not profess to be followers of Christ. In other words, there will be some unsaved in that day. Surely they will constitute a small minority, but still they will live and be apt subjects for Satan's final influence. How early in the thousand-year period any unsaved persons will exist, one can only guess. It will not be at the very beginning, for then only saved people will be permitted to enter the period. But as children are born, some will eventually show this rebellion, even though they will be outside the normal pattern of life in doing so. That this will occur, in such a day as the millennium, shows significantly how desperately wicked the heart of man is by nature (Jer. 17:9).

4. *The dwelling place of glorified saints*

The dwelling place of glorified saints during the millennium is not easily settled. Will it be here on earth, where living saints will have their homes? Living saints will indeed have homes, much as now, conducting their lives in the same general pattern. But will glorified saints live in this manner? Those of amillennial persuasion, assuming that this is the view of premillennialists, have been critical in this regard. For instance, G. L. Murray writes, "Premillennialism makes no provision for the reconciliation of such irreconcilables as resurrected saints and mortal sinners in the same society." [8] It is then necessary to consider the question. While the following considerations do not give a certain answer, they do offer guidance for thinking and show the impropriety of the criticism just noted.

a. Resurrected saints and living saints may live together. The thought of resurrected saints and "mortal sinners" living together is not irreconcilable. Though all premillennialists do not believe that the two groups will dwell on earth together, the thought of them doing so is not absurd, as Murray implies. It is noteworthy that Christ, in His glorified body, lived on earth during the forty days which elapsed between His resurrection and ascension. He ate with His disciples (Luke 24:30; John 21:12-15) and carried on numerous conversations with people. Also, Old Testament saints, who rose from the dead at the same general time as He, lived here on earth for a time. It is not likely that glorified saints will live in homes, at least in family situations, as do living saints; for they will not marry (Matt. 22:30) or have children. God, however, could provide the type of dwelling which would suit their needs.

---

[8] G. L. Murray, *Millennial Studies,* p. 91.

b. The New Jerusalem as the dwelling place. Some premillennialists believe that the New Jerusalem will be this dwelling place, provided by God. They think of the New Jerusalem being located in the atmosphere, slightly above the earth, and visible to earth's inhabitants. Pentecost, who favors the view, argues for it in the following vein. [9] He shows, first, that the purpose of the millennium, in that it pertains to living saints rather than glorified, would still be served if the glorified saints did live apart from the earth in this manner. Second, the inhabitants of the New Jerusalem, as implied in its description (Rev. 21), will include representatives of all ages and therefore would qualify as a home for all glorified saints, who come from all ages. Third, biblical heroes of faith looked for a "city," which he believes could well be this New Jerusalem (see Gal. 4:26; Heb. 11:10, 16; 12:22-24; Rev. 3:12; 21:2, 10); and so their living in the New Jerusalem during the millennium could be the fulfillment of this expectancy.

The view has appeal, for it answers several questions. If glorified saints should dwell in this "city," near to living saints but still not among them, the matter of an appropriate place for them would be solved. They would be near at hand for aiding in the rule of the earth. Further, the disparity in numbers between glorified saints and living saints, especially at the beginning of the millennium, would be less apparent. There is some difficulty, however, in the lack of evidence that the New Jerusalem, as described in Revelation 21, will exist as early as the millennial day. The first nine verses of the chapter quite clearly refer only to the eternal state, which follows the millennium, and no exegetical reason exists for understanding the verses following any differently. To hold that it does exist during the millennial period, then, is only on the basis of supposition, not scriptural statement.

c. Heaven as the dwelling place. Still another explanation is offered by McClain, [10] who believes that heaven will be the millennial abode of glorified saints. He sees the vast distance between heaven and earth as presenting no problem, since the glorified body has the power of instantaneous movement. Glorified saints would be able to live in heaven, he believes, and still have access to the earth to serve in whatever ruling capacities were assigned. He cites no Scripture as evidence, but seems to argue

---

[9] J. Dwight Pentecost, *Things To Come,* pp. 532-546.
[10] Alva J. McClain, *The Greatness of the Kingdom,* pp. 500-502.

on the basis of available possibilities and believes the most likely is found here.

d. Conclusion. A final, certain answer is not forthcoming. The Scriptures simply do not say where glorified saints will live. Any of the three suggestions made, however, qualify as possibilities.

D. Worship

One of the most basic features of the millennium is the matter of worship, as it will then be observed. What place will worship hold during the millennium, and what form will it take?

1. *Worship will be important*

A point amillennialists often make is that the kingdom they present is spiritual in nature, whereas that of premillennialists is materialistic and earthly. [11] In view of this thinking, it is important to make clear that, though the millennial kingdom does concern the material realities of earth, it is at the same time characterized by true spirituality. The worship of God plays a major role. Recognition of this truth follows logically from the idea of the period, as outlined earlier. If the millennium is the realization of God's true rule over His earthly creation, including the hearts of men, then true worship, the necessary response of subjects to such a rule, must result.

It is for this reason that only true followers of God are permitted to enter the period and that the Holy Spirit is poured out on mankind, as set forth in Joel 2:28, 29. [12] With Christ ruling, an atmosphere will be established which will be conducive to this manner of worship. Worship of God will be a factor in the life of millennial inhabitants to a marked extent. It will no doubt be of greater degree and genuineness than at any time since the Garden of Eden (see Isa. 12:1-6; 25:1 - 26:19; 56:7; 61:10, 11; 66:23; Jer. 33:11; Ezek. 20:40, 41; 40:1 - 46:24; Zech. 6:12-15; 8:20-23; 14:16-21).

2. *Christ as Priest-King*

The Scriptures present Christ in the role of Priest as well as King, during this time. In other words, He will serve as spiritual leader, as well as political. Zechariah says, "Behold the man

---

[11] See, for example, O. T. Allis, *Prophecy and the Church,* pp. 69-71.
[12] See above, pp. 163, 164 for discussion.

whose name is The BRANCH; . . . he shall sit and rule upon his throne; and he shall be a priest upon his throne" (6:12, 13). And in the eschatological context of Psalm 110, Christ is referred to by the words, "Thou art a priest for ever after the order of Melchizedek" (v. 4). It was God's intention even in Old Testament time that He, as God, should serve as both civil and religious head of His people. He gave His Law on Mt. Sinai on this basis, structuring it to cover both areas of life. With sin abounding as it does in the world today, there is wisdom in maintaining a distinction between church and state, but this is not the ideal. With Christ as supreme head, the ideal can and will be realized. The difficulties in separating the two areas, encountered so frequently in the present time, will thus be removed. No secular areas will be permitted to exist without the proper influence of the religious.

3. *The religious leadership of Israel*

The nation of Israel will take the lead for the world in rendering true worship to God. Israel's citizens will be limited to those who will have been "refined" and "tried" (Zech. 13:8, 9), as noted earlier, and they will provide an example of what true worship means. God desired His people to provide a similar example in the days of the Old Testament. This is the significance of His words to them from Mt. Sinai: "Ye shall be unto me a kingdom of priests" (Exod. 19:6). Isaiah uses similar language concerning the millennium, saying of Israel, "But ye shall be named the Priests of the LORD: men shall call you the ministers of our God" (61:6). The prophet asserts that the Gentiles, in turn, will recognize them in this capacity: "All that see them shall acknowledge them, that they are the seed which the LORD hath blessed (61:9).

4. *Worship among the Gentiles*

With Israel taking the lead in worshiping God during the millennium, and with Jerusalem being the religious center of the world, Gentile worship could be expected also to be oriented toward Palestine. This is where Christ, the object of worship, will be. Isaiah describes the glory of Christ in Israel at the time, and then states, "And the Gentiles shall come to thy light, and kings to the brightness of thy rising" (60:3). Later he speaks of Jerusalem's gates being open continuously, that men may bring unto Christ "the forces of the Gentiles. . . . For "the nation and kingdom that will not serve [Christ] shall perish" (60:11, 12; cf. Zech. 8:22, 23). A strong desire will exist to visit Jerusalem, with people saying, "Let us go up to the mountain of the LORD, to the house of the God of Jacob; and he will teach us of his ways, and we will walk in his paths" (Isa. 2:3). Visits of this kind will be possible through the remarkable means of transportation now existent, which will then probably be even more rapid and convenient.

In their home countries, of course, Gentiles will be expected to worship as well. The Scriptures give little direct information to help in this connection, but certainly God will expect true faith to be expressed in prayer and the reading of His Word. There will be need for continuous heartfelt adoration of God and attention to witnessing to any wayward people one may know. Though local churches should not be expected to exist, since the invisible church will then be totally in glorified form, still there may be occasions of meeting for the purpose of collective worship. God will be pleased with all means of rendering glory unto Himself.

5. *Millennial temple and sacrifices*

Still to be discussed is the subject of the millennial temple and sacrifices. Will there be a temple during the millennium, and will animals again be killed in sacrifice there? Amillennialists charge that the establishment of a literal temple again, with a sacrificial system, would be a serious retrogression from the glory of the Gospel. They point out, quite correctly, that the typical rites and ceremonies of the Old Testament religious program found their greater reality in the Gospel. Even some premillennialists hold back on a literal interpretation in respect to this matter. It may be noted in passing, too, that simply because a temple and sacrifices will exist during the tribulation period does not mean that the same will be true in the millennium. If these do exist during the millennium, their place and purpose will be quite different than during the tribulation. The tribulation temple will be built on the site of the Old Testament temples, but according to Ezekiel's description in chapters 40 - 46, the millennium temple will not be located in exactly the same place. Also, it is quite possible that the Antichrist will have destroyed the earlier temple by the time of the millennium.

There are a number of scripture passages, however, which

do speak of a temple and sacrifices existing, and their contexts are clearly millennial in character. Among these are the following: Isaiah 56:6-8; 66:21; Jeremiah 33:15-18; Ezekiel 20:40, 41; 40:1 - 46:24; Zechariah 14:16. If these references are to be taken literally, which a basic tenet of premillennialism requires, then the existence of both temple and sacrifices in the millennium must be accepted. Three factors call for discussion.

a. The temple described in Ezekiel 40 - 48. In Ezekiel 40 - 48, a temple and ceremonial system are described at considerable length. Are they the temple and ceremonial system of the millennium? Most premillennialists, who do believe that both a temple and sacrifices will exist during the period, accept the idea that they are.

Among expositors who do not accept the idea, most adhere to one of two alternative interpretations. The first is that Ezekiel describes an ideal temple, which the Jews should have built after the return from captivity but did not. In response, however, one cannot help but wonder why so much place should be given in God's Word to a description which was never to be fulfilled. The second is that this temple symbolizes the spiritual blessings of the church. But this interpretation seems unlikely because advocates are unable to explain the symbolism in any detail. The reason is that the symbolism does not fit church truth. This leaves the interpretation which does believe that a literal temple and sacrifices of the millennial day are set forth.

No building has ever been built like the one described, which means that, if the description is to be taken literally, it would have to be still future. Besides this, Ezekiel gives two helpful clues which indicate that he is depicting the millennial temple and sacrifices. First, he includes in his description a picture of the "glory of the LORD" entering into this temple, which implies an identification with the glory which he had previously seen departing from the temple of his day (43:1-5; cf. 11:23). Second, the prophet hears the voice of God saying that this temple is "the place of my throne, and the place of the soles of my feet, where I will dwell in the midst of the children of Israel for ever" (43:7). Still a third clue may be taken from the very length and detail given to the description. This says quite definitely that the building and system being described are of major importance, an importance which would be uniquely true of a millennial temple and system.

b. Sacrifices in the millennium. The most frequent objection to the idea of a temple in the millennium concerns the matter of sacrifices. The argument is that Christ abolished the Old Testament sacrificial system, which makes such a reestablishment absurd and impossible. A response may be given to this, however. Christ did abolish the system, but only in the sense that it prefigured His complete expiatory work for sin. He did not abolish the idea of symbols, for today both the Lord's Supper and Baptism are based on this idea. The thought of symbolism for sacrifices, then, could well still continue, only with the symbolism changed. Rather than picturing the sacrifice of Christ as still to be provided, they could depict it as having occurred. In this capacity, the sacrifices would fill basically the same role as is now done by the Lord's Supper and Baptism. The latter were given to the church as memorial observances. The sacrifices would then be given to the Jews as the same. And would not sacrifices be altogether appropriate to serve in this way for the Jews, who had used them to picture so realistically Christ's death beforehand?

c. Some objections considered. Certain objections are raised against this view. Response has already been given to a main one, namely that certain scripture passages show that any reestablishment of sacrifices would be unnecessary and improper. Among such passages are Hebrews 7:27 and 9:12, 26, which speak of Christ having offered the final sacrifice to God. If the sacrifices are taken as memorials, however, and not prefigurements, this objection vanishes. Another objection is taken from such a passage as Ephesians 2:14-16. Here, the barrier between Jew and Gentile is said to have been broken down by Christ. The thought is that the reestablishment of a distinctly Jewish temple and system would raise that barrier again. To this we may reply, first, that such a passage presents God's purpose for the church age, rather than the millennial period; and, second, that even during the millennium the thought of this verse is not really contradicted. For, though sacrificing would be from the background of Jewish history and would be administered by Jews, still Gentiles would be very welcome to commemorate Christ's death in this way as well. Zechariah states directly that Gentiles will "go up from year to year to worship the King" (14:16). Both Jews and Gentiles would share in this form of worship.

A third objection is that it will be geographically impossible to bring about the worship described by Ezekiel. Particularly, it is said that the environs of the temple, as described by the prophet, are much larger than those of the ancient temple area (Ezek. 45:1-6). This point is correct; but offsetting its force are two factors. First, some important topographical changes will occur in the area of Jerusalem by the beginning of the millennium, which could have a bearing on the size and availability of temple area. For instance, the Mount of Olives will split open, making a valley running through it from east to west (Zech. 14:4). [13] Second, the exact location of the millennial temple will probably be somewhat different from that of ancient time, though certainly still near Jerusalem, which is so often described as the religious center of the land.

A fourth objection is that the view minimizes the place of the cross and even restricts its value to the present age. This, however, is not a correct assertion. Those who enter the millennial age will have been saved by faith in Christ's finished work on the cross; their descendants will be saved on the same basis. In fact, as already noted, the sacrifices will be memorials of Christ's atonement made on the cross.

6. *The nature of millennial worship*

The principal matters in the foregoing discussion may be summarized in the following points. First, salvation during the millennium will be by faith in Christ's finished work of atonement, just as today. Second, worship by all the saved will be basically the same as today, through the exercise of faith in and the adoration of God. Third, because the majority of people will be saved, and because a knowledge of and interest in the things of God will be normal, there will be no need of an organization like the church today. Rather, people will worship out of sincere hearts as a daily experience, wherever they are. Fourth, because Christ the King will rule out of Jerusalem and because memorial sacrifices will be conducted at the temple, the natural desire will be to go there frequently for special occasions of worship. Rapid means of transportation existent today may be made even more efficient and convenient by that time, to facilitate the necessary travel.

---

[13] Significant "signs" occur at the close of the tribulation (Matt. 24:29), which may even include a mighty earthquake (Rev. 16:18-20), and these could cause changes also.

Questions for Review

1. What is the basic reason for the millennium, in respect to the world at large?
2. What is the basic reason for the millennium, in respect to the Jews?
3. What are some ideals of life that will be realized during the millennium? Cite Scripture for each one.
4. What key passage speaks of the outpouring of the Holy Spirit during the millennium?
5. What are some results that will come from this outpouring?
6. Cite Scriptures which show that peace and social justice will be enjoyed during the millennium.
7. What are some physical benefits that will be experienced during the millennium?
8. How long will the millennial reign of Christ last? Give scriptural evidence.
9. In what sense will the kingdom continue for all eternity?
10. Cite passages which show that Christ will serve as King during the millennium,
11. List arguments which show that Jeremiah 30:9 (and other "David" passages) refer to the historical David as being ruler over Israel during the millennium.
12. Set forth answers which may be given to these arguments.
13. Describe Christ's rule over Israel during the millennium.
14. Describe Christ's rule over Gentiles during the millennium.
15. What passages indicate that glorified saints will rule with Christ?
16. How will the numbers of glorified saints and normal living saints compare at the beginning of the millennium? at its end?
17. Will all glorified saints reign with Christ? Explain.
18. Cite scriptural evidence that sin will exist during the millennium.
19. What three answers may be given as to the possible dwelling place of glorified saints during the millennium? Discuss.
20. How important will worship of God be in the millennium?
21. Will there be a separation of church and state during the millennium? Explain.
22. What nation will take the lead in worship during the millennium?

23. Describe the manner of worship of Gentiles during the millennium.
24. Will the same temple exist during the millennium as during the tribulation?
25. What temple is described in Ezekiel 40 - 48? Give evidence for your answer.
26. What objections are raised to the idea of sacrifices during the millennium?
27. What answers can be given to these objections?
28. In your own words, summarize principal features of millennial worship.

Bibliography

Allis, Oswald T. *Prophecy and the Church.* Philadelphia: Presbyterian and Reformed Publishing Co., 1945.

Anderson, Robert. *The Coming Prince.* London: Hodder and Stoughton, 1909.

Andrews, Samuel J. *Christianity and Anti-Christianity in Their Final Conflict.* Chicago: The Bible Institute Colportage Association, 1898.

Barnes, Albert. *Daniel.* 2 vols. Notes on the Old Testament, edited by Robert Few. Grand Rapids: Baker Book House, 1950.

_____. *Revelation.* Notes on the New Testament. Grand Rapids: Eerdmans Publishing Co., 1966.

Blackstone, W. E. *Jesus Is Coming.* New York: Fleming H. Revell Co., 1908.

Boettner, Loraine. *The Millennium.* Philadelphia: Presbyterian and Reformed Publishing Co., 1958.

Boutflower, Charles. *In and Around the Book of Daniel.* London: Society for Promoting Christian Knowledge, 1923.

Calvin, John. *Commentaries on the Book of the Prophet Daniel.* Translated by Thomas Myers, 2 vols. Edinburgh: Calvin Translation Society, 1852.

Chafer, Lewis Sperry. *Systematic Theology.* 8 vols. Grand Rapids: Zondervan Publishing House, 1947.

Charles, Robert H. *The Book of Daniel.* The New Century Bible, edited by Walter F. Adeney. New York: H. Frowde, Oxford University Press, n.d.

Culver, Robert D. *Daniel and the Latter Days.* Chicago: Moody Press, 1965.

Darby, J. N., *Synopsis of the Books of the Bible.* 5 vols. London: G. Morrish, n.d.

DeHaan, M. R. *The Jew and Palestine in Prophecy.* Grand Rapids: Zondervan Publishing House, 1950.

DeHaan, Richard W. *Israel and the Nations in Prophecy.* Grand Rapids: Zondervan Publishing House, 1968.

English, E. Schuyler. *Re-Thinking the Rapture*. New York: Loizeaux Brothers, 1970.

Feinberg, Charles. *Premillennialism or Amillennialism?* Grand Rapids: Zondervan Publishing House, 1936.

Gaebelein, Arno C. *Hopeless Yet There Is Hope*. New York: Our Hope, 1935.

————. *The Prophet Daniel*. New York: Our Hope, 1911.

————. *The Prophet Ezekiel*. New York: Our Hope, 1918.

Gray, James M. *Prophecy and the Lord's Return*. New York: Fleming H. Revell Co., 1917.

Haldeman, I. M. *The Signs of the Times*. New York: Charles C. Cook, 1916.

Hamilton, Floyd. *The Basis of Millennial Faith*. Grand Rapids: Wm. B. Eerdmans Publishing Co., 1942.

Hamilton, Gavin. *Will the Church Escape the Great Tribulation?* New York: Loizeaux Brothers, 1941.

Harrison, Norman B. *The End*. Minneapolis: Harrison Service, 1941.

Hendriksen, William. *And So All Israel Shall Be Saved*. Grand Rapids: Baker Book House, 1945.

Hogg, C. F. and W. E. Vine. *The Church and the Tribulation*. London: Pickering and Inglis, n.d.

————. *The Epistles to the Thessalonians*. London: Alfred Holness, n.d.

Ironside, Henry A. *The Great Parenthesis*. New York: Loizeaux Brothers, 1943.

————. *Lectures on Daniel the Prophet*. New York: Loizeaux Brothers, 1953.

————. *Lectures on the Revelation*. New York: Loizeaux Brothers, 1953.

Jennings, F. C. *Studies in Revelation*. New York: Loizeaux Brothers, n.d.

Keil, Carl Friedrich. *Daniel*. Translated by M. G. Easton. Commentaries on the Old Testament. 25 vols. Grand Rapids: Wm. B. Eerdmans Publishing Co., 1952.

————. *Ezekiel*. Translated by James Martin. 2 vols. Commentaries on the Old Testament. 25 vols. Grand Rapids: Wm. B. Eerdmans Publishing Co., 1952.

Kelly, William. *Lectures on the Book of Daniel*. New York: Loizeaux Brothers, n.d.

————. *Lectures on the Revelation*. London: G. Morrish, n.d.

King, Geoffrey R. *Daniel.* Grand Rapids: Wm. B. Eerdmans Publishing Co., 1967.

Kromminga, D. H. *The Millennium in the Church.* Grand Rapids: Wm. B. Eerdmans Publishing Co., 1948.

Ladd, George E. *The Blessed Hope.* Grand Rapids: Wm. B. Eerdmans Publishing Co., 1956.

_____. *Crucial Questions About the Kingdom of God.* Grand Rapids: Wm. B. Eerdmans Publishing Co., 1952.

_____. *The Gospel of the Kingdom.* Grand Rapids: Wm. B. Eerdmans Publishing Co., 1959.

Larkin, Clarence. *Dispensational Truth or God's Plan and Purpose in the Ages.* Philadelphia: Rev. Clarence Larkin, 1920.

_____. *The Book of Daniel.* Philadelphia: Rev. Clarence Larkin, 1929.

Leupold, Herbert C. *Exposition of Daniel.* Grand Rapids: Baker Book House, 1969.

McClain, Alva J. *Daniel's Prophecy of the Seventy Weeks.* Grand Rapids: Zondervan Publishing House, 1940.

_____. *The Greatness of the Kingdom.* Chicago: Moody Press, 1968.

Masselink, William. *Why Thousand Years?* Grand Rapids: Wm. B. Eerdmans Publishing Co., 1930.

Mauro, Philip. *After This.* New York: Fleming H. Revell, 1918.

_____. *The Patmos Visions.* Boston: Hamilton Bros., 1925.

Montgomery, James A. *A Critical and Exegetical Commentary on the Book of Daniel.* The International Critical Commentary. New York: Charles Scribner's Sons, 1927.

Morris, Leon. *The First and Second Epistles to the Thessalonians.* New International Commentary of the New Testament. Grand Rapids: Wm. B. Eerdmans Publishing Co., 1959.

Murray, George L. *Millennial Studies.* Grand Rapids: Baker Book House, 1948.

Newell, William R. *The Book of the Revelation.* Chicago: Moody Press, 1935.

_____. *Daniel: The Man Greatly Beloved and His Prophecies.* Chicago: Moody Press, 1962.

Olmstead, A. T. *History of Assyria.* Chicago: University of Chicago Press, 1960.

Pache, Rene. *The Return of Jesus Christ.* Translated by William S. LaSor. Chicago: Moody Press, 1955.

Pentecost, J. Dwight. *Prophecy for Today.* Grand Rapids: Zondervan Publishing House, 1961.

_____ . *Things to Come.* Grand Rapids: Zondervan Publishing House, 1958.

Peters, George N. H. *The Theocratic Kingdom.* 3 vols. Grand Rapids: Kregel Publications, 1952.

Pettingill, William. *Simple Studies in the Revelation.* Wilmington, Delaware: Just A Word, Inc., n.d.

Pfeiffer, C., ed. *The Biblical World: A Dictionary of Biblical Archaeology.* Grand Rapids: Baker Book House, 1964.

Pink, Arthur W. *The Antichrist.* Swengel, Pa.: Bible Truth Depot, 1923.

Pusey, Edward B. *Daniel the Prophet.* New York: Funk & Wagnalls, 1885.

Reese, Alexander. *The Approaching Advent of Christ.* London: Marshall, Morgan and Scott, n.d.

Rutgers, William H. *Premillennialism in America.* Goes, Holland: Oosterbaan & Le Cointre, 1930.

Ryrie, Charles C. *The Basis of the Premillennial Faith.* New York: Loizeaux Brothers, 1954.

_____ . *The Bible and Tomorrow's News.* Wheaton: Scripture Press, 1969.

Saggs, H. W. F. *The Greatness That Was Babylon.* New York: Praeger Publishers, Inc., 1968.

Saphir, Adolph. *Christ and Israel.* London: Morgan & Scott, 1911.

Scofield, Cyrus I., ed. *The Scofield Reference Bible.* New York: Oxford University Press, 1909.

_____ . *What Do the Prophets Say?* Philadelphia: The Sunday School Times Co., 1916.

Scott, Walter. *Exposition of the Revelation of Jesus Christ.* London: Pickering and Inglis, n.d.

Seiss, Joseph. *The Apocalypse.* 3 vols. 11th ed. New York: Charles C. Cook, 1913.

Smith, Wilbur. *World Crises and the Prophetic Scriptures.* Chicago: Moody Press, 1951.

Stanton, Gerald B. *Kept From the Hour.* Grand Rapids: Zondervan Publishing House, 1956.

Stevens, W. C. *Revelation, the Crown-Jewel of Prophecy.* 2 vols. New York: Christian Alliance Publishing Co., 1928.

Strauss, Lehman. *The Prophecies of Daniel.* Neptune, N.J.: Loizeaux Brothers, 1969.

Trench, Richard F. *Synonyms of the New Testament.* 12th ed. London: Kegan, Paul, Trench, Trubner, and Co., Ltd., 1894.

Urquhart, John. *The Wonders of Prophecy.* 6th. ed. Boston: Hamilton Bros., n.d.

Walvoord, John F. *Daniel the Key to Prophetic Revelation.* Chicago: Moody Press, 1971.

_____. *Israel in Prophecy.* Grand Rapids: Zondervan Publishing House, 1962.

_____. *The Millennial Kingdom.* Grand Rapids: Zondervan Publishing House, 1959.

_____. *The Nations in Prophecy.* Grand Rapids: Zondervan Publishing House, 1967.

_____. *The Rapture Question.* Grand Rapids: Zondervan Publishing House, 1970.

_____. *The Revelation of Jesus Christ.* Chicago: Moody Press, 1966.

_____. *The Thessalonian Epistles.* Grand Rapids: Zondervan Publishing House, 1958.

Wilson, Robert Dick. *Studies in the Book of Daniel.* New York: G. P. Putnam's Sons, 1917.

Wood, Leon J. *Is the Rapture Next?* Grand Rapids: Zondervan Publishing House, 1956.

_____. *A Commentary on Daniel.* Grand Rapids: Zondervan Publishing House, 1973.

Wyngaarden, Martin J. *The Future of the Kingdom in Prophecy and Fulfillment.* Grand Rapids: Zondervan Publishing House, 1934.

Young, Edward J. *The Prophecy of Daniel.* Grand Rapids: Wm. B. Eerdmans Publishing Co., 1949.

Zockler, Otto. *The Book of the Prophet Daniel.* A Commentary on the Holy Scriptures, edited by John P. Lange, vol. 13. New York: Charles Scribner's Sons, 1915.

Scripture

Index

Subject
Index